Praise for *Hallowed Ground*

"*Hallowed Ground* is a poignant, humor-filled narrative that unpacks the complexity of age, aging, and the aged inside American families. Deeply personal and seasoned with Southern charm, Minnix reflects on his decades of service and gives practical advice for living well regardless of age, health, and ability."

—Gretchen E. Alkema, PhD,
Next Avenue, "2017 Influencer in Aging"

"As a pioneer in the field of geriatrics, Dr. Larry Minnix has occupied a front row seat to observe, empathize, and understand the challenges of aging. His keen insight and sharp wit are displayed in this authentic collection of experiences as only a person with his care and concern can relay. A must-read for every age!"

—Lillian Budd Darden

"You'll laugh. You'll cry, and you'll scratch your head in amazement. Larry Minnix has—through gifted story-telling—captured many truths about aging, families, adult children, and compassionate individuals who work on their behalf. As societies grow older, we need the important reminders, woven through these stories, of the human dimension of this massive demographic change and the significant challenges and opportunities that they present."

—Katie Smith Sloan, Present and CEO, LeadingAge

Hallowed Ground

Stories of Successful Aging

Larry Minnix

Hallowed Ground: Stories of Successful Aging

Published by Wheatmark®
2030 East Speedway Boulevard, Suite 106
Tucson, Arizona 85719 USA
www.wheatmark.com

ISBN: 978-1-62787-626-1 (paperback)
ISBN: 978-1-62787-627-8 (ebook)
LCCN: 2018906831

This book is dedicated to my wife, Kathleen. She is beyond cliché labels like "inspiration," "partner," "love of my life." She is much more. In fact, she is one of the few people I have met in my life that is an old soul and has given me access to wisdom of the ages.

Recently I heard a presentation by an Emory oncologist named Dr. Bill Eley. The discussion surrounding his topic led to the impact of spiritual health on fighting cancer. He acknowledged the power of it in mystical, immeasurable ways. In the course of that discussion, he asserted his belief that we become an accumulation of the great souls we have encountered in our lives, which is another way to think about the afterlife.

Embedded in Kathleen is a repository of saints from which I benefit every day and through which I became sensitive to hallowed ground in people's lives. I hope that if you read this book, you will be enlightened by countless souls who have prepared hallowed ground for you.

—Larry Minnix

A Note to the Reader

This book is drawn from my personal experience and from four decades spent in a career in aging services. The stories I tell are true to the best of my recollection, though sometimes names are changed and circumstances disguised.

I frequently refer to the two great organizations that employed me in leadership capacities, including the CEO position in both. The first is Wesley Woods, a comprehensive nonprofit senior services organization founded by the North Georgia Conference of the United Methodist Church and Emory University. The Towers is a Wesley Woods independent living community. Budd Terrace is an intermediate care nursing home. The Health Center was a skilled nursing home now out of business, and the Wesley Woods Hospital specializes in geriatrics.

LeadingAge is an association of not-for-profit senior services organizations and related businesses and professionals, based in

Washington, DC. It offers professional development, applied research, and advocacy services.

I was associated with Wesley Woods for twenty-eight years, the last ten as CEO. I succeeded my mentor and friend there, the late J. Scott Houston, when he retired in 1990. I became CEO of (what is now called) LeadingAge in 2001 and held that position for the last fifteen years of my career.

I am also grateful to the Decatur First United Methodist Church of the North Georgia Annual Conference. Many of the personal situations that inspired this book emanated from my church. In addition, the Wesleyan tradition of ministry has been encouraging of specialized ministries like mine, which attempt to serve people far beyond the boundaries of the traditional parish. I am eternally grateful to these organizations for their confidence in me and for providing unusual environments in which to experience hallowed ground.

And a special thanks to Judith Vera-Barra and Jim Berklan for their expert editing advice.

Contents

Contents

Introduction

"...the last act will test the play..."

"The last act has begun, and it will test the play." This quote comes from Malcolm Cowley's book *The View from 80*, and I heard it in 1981 from Dr. Marvin Rast, a retired minister living at Wesley Woods, where my career in aging services began. Even as a young executive, when he told me this, the truth of that statement struck me. Today, at seventy, it resonates even more deeply. I am now in that "last act" myself. I will be tested.

How do we age successfully? How do we make our own play end well? Erik Erikson, a great psychologist of the twentieth century, detailed "eight ages" of life's development. Each "age" has a basic conflict to be addressed internally. The outcome of that conflict shapes how each of us approaches life in subsequent ages.

Infants face the conflict of "trust versus mistrust." Toddlers emerge either believing that they can trust their environment and the people in it or they cannot. Trust builds self-confidence and a constructive outlook on life. Mistrust leads to melancholy, broken relationships, and a host of social ills.

In late middle age, the conflict is between "generativity versus stagnation." In traditional retirement, will I be productive or vegetate? Will I remain engaged with other people or detach and become depressed? The last phase of life, "ego integrity versus despair," raises the question Has my life been worthwhile? If it has, that attitude influences whether society treats me with dignity or disdain and whether my family remembers me fondly or resentfully.

Perhaps the biblical characters of Abraham and Sarah are our archetype of successful aging. God asked them late in life if they would do something really *big* for humankind, like be the father and mother of many nations—no small task. Sarah laughed and said they were too old, an understandable response. God countered with something like: "I didn't ask you how old you are. I asked if you'd do a *big* job." They did, and the rest is history. The Bible says they died at "a good old age," with family, friends, and the trappings of their fruitful lives around them. (Admittedly, I have taken liberty with the dialogue between God, Abraham, and Sarah reflected in more traditional translations.)

A good old age! Most of us would aspire to that. Yet we often fear and fight the process and die with unfinished business—psychological, spiritual, financial—which leaves others with regret, guilt, and blame. But a good old age leads to a good death with few regrets. Families and friends grieve but rejoice in a life well lived, a life whose positive impact will be felt for years to come.

I have come to believe that aging has a fulfilling purpose in life. If it didn't, our Creator would have constructed the process of living and dying differently. I believe God wants us to have a good old age with few, if any, regrets.

Therefore, I am writing this book for three reasons.

First, I believe it is my calling to do so. I have known too many families who have lived what one dear friend calls "Old People

Hell," a torment that lasted the last decade of her parents' lives and led to family tensions and sleepless nights that endure today. Out of my fifty years of experience in the mental health and aging care professions, as well as personal relationships, I have come to believe that Old People Hell can be avoided or even transformed into a good old age through the illustration of power shown by the stories I am about to tell.

Ken Durand is my longtime friend and colleague in the field of aging services. He wrote me once about the raison d'être of the work he and I shared. He said, "This old age is not only worthwhile but it is meant to be. Therefore, it is our responsibility to help people get the most out of it." Yes, I feel that responsibility.

Second, I want to tell *my* story. My family is not known for great achievement or famous personalities, but our saga is both ordinary *and* unique. It is filled with humor and pathos, love and abuse, good and evil people, wise and stupid choices, failure and success. There are family members who went to prison and others who made a success of their lives. Some dropped out of school, while others earned advanced degrees and taught and even founded educational institutions. Some who dropped out of school established successful enterprises. I hope to convey the importance of knowing your own family story.

Third, I write this so that I will generate and not stagnate. If this book helps a few people, then I am productive beyond formal retirement. I can feel that my life has been worthwhile. I can die at a good old age and leave my family with no regrets about our relationship.

I think of the stories you are about to read as "hallowed ground." Moses stood on hallowed ground when he received the command from the burning bush to lead His people. I define hallowed ground as the intersection of powerful human experience with divine messages. I have often stood on hallowed ground with people who have shared their stories with me, stories borne of illness and conflict or overcoming obstacles and triumphant transformations.

Through these stories, I want to convey what I call the secrets of successful aging. The following is a summary of those secrets. The rest of the book will be filled with stories that bring them to life. I tell stories because I heard an expert say that people retain a small percentage of the PowerPoint data they hear but a large percentage of the stories they are told. Maya Angelou said, "I've learned that people will forget what you said, people will forget what you did, but people will never forget how you made them feel." Stories make us feel. Stories have been how truth has been passed down through the generations, long before there was the written word.

I hope these stories will evoke feelings—feelings that generate insights for successful aging from people who have learned those secrets by living them.

The Twelve Secrets

"... to shrivel or expand..."

As I traveled around the country meeting older people, their family members, and staff who cared for them, I often wondered what makes the difference in how a person grows old. Why does one person shrivel in their soul as they shrivel in their body while another expands spiritually even as their body shrinks?

Emblazoned in my memory is the Reverend Roy McTier at age 101, praising God at the top of his feeble lungs encased in his remaining bony body as he lay dying in a state-of-the-art hospital at Emory. I walked in on him as he seemed to be shrieking in pain. Instead, he was praising God. Where does that zest for life and the adoration for the eternal Giver of it come from?

Based on my observations, I have concluded that there are twelve secrets of successful aging embodied in people like Roy. The stories that follow illustrate these twelve secrets in subsequent chapters. There is some research scattered throughout the professional literature to support these secrets. Perhaps the best summary of that research is in the book *Successful Aging* by the eminent Dr. John Rowe. I recommend it to you.

1. CHOOSE YOUR ANCESTORS WISELY—AND GET TO KNOW THEM. Beyond genetics, understand your family history and dynamics. Crazy Aunt Lucy who no one talks about may have had an untreated bipolar disorder that runs in your family. My own family had alcoholics, gamblers, and abusers. That fact has informed what I have told my children about addiction. Understanding your genes and your family history can help future generations keep out of serious trouble, as well as help you understand your own body and mind.

2. MANAGE YOUR LIFESTYLE. This is hard for me because I have always struggled with my weight, though usually not hard enough. My mother used to reassure me I just had big bones, but I know I have a big appetite, one often triggered by stress. Successful aging is associated with choices about food, habits, activities, the management of anger, healthy relationships, and the management of the health challenges that inevitably arise because of genetic flaws and accidents.

3. CULTIVATE AN ATTITUDE OF PERSEVERANCE. Successful aging reflects successful living. Aging begins at conception and ends at death. It includes predictable cycles, each with its own opportunities and challenges, losses and gains, successes and failures. Even the challenges can produce wisdom. Don't ask, "Why *me?*" Ask, "What can I learn from this? What can I teach?" Resist the stereotypical view of aging as peaking at forty, then declining until death, augmented by Botox, implants, chemicals, and trophy partners.

   There is no fountain of youth, but there are successful

strategies for fulfillment as we age. There are three basic old-age personas from which to choose: Victim, as characterized by disease, decline, and dependence; Denier, as characterized by artificial trappings and avoidance; and Perseverance, characterized by acceptance of aging and the adaptations needed to make the most of it. Yes, there are genuine victims among us: truly helpless people. We have a moral duty to them. But deniers create difficulty for us because they choose to succumb to their pride and stubbornness. Perseverance is the third choice, based on attitude. Roy persevered.

4. AVOID GIVING ORGAN RECITALS. Don't talk about your innards and whether or not they are working properly. People do not enjoy your "organ recitals," as my dear friend Harold called them. They create self-fulfilling prophesies, decreased self-confidence, and social isolation. You are not an accumulation of your diseases. Yes, it is important to keep your loved ones informed about your health. Just don't talk about it all the time! Don't become your diseases. You are not an arthritic or a bipolar. You are a person who happens to have been dealt that hand.

5. CULTIVATE INTIMACY. Intimate encounters occur in the confession booth, around the dinner table, traveling to and from school with the grandkids, and in the bedroom. It happens through massage, hugs, sharing secrets, bedside visitation in the nursing home, Bible study groups, and orgasm. Don't let growing older confine you inside a dismal bubble. If your spouse has died, use bereavement as an opportunity to learn from your previous marriage to make the next one better or to just be grateful for the life you led together. But don't isolate yourself. My wife, Kathleen, has often said that

if she predeceases me, she is confident that I will have one eye open, scanning the assembled crowd, looking for rich widows to replace her at the final graveside prayer. She's said she hopes I'd remarry.

6. LAUGH AND PLAY. I believe that inside every eighty-five-year-old is the remnant of a delightfully immature young-ster. Find the humor in life—especially in the most difficult situations. Belly laughs create cathartic body chemistry. The creative arts, naughty stories, parlor games, trips, and lifelong learning are mediums for play and laughter. Laughter and play remind us that we are still alive, not merely waiting to die. As Camus said, "In the midst of winter, I found that there was, within me, an invincible summer."

7. AVOID POISONOUS PEOPLE. Some people are turds in life's punchbowl. Some are even evil. Some are just downers. Some make you a lightning rod for their hostility. Others are leeches. Some are carriers of stress, and stress is as contagious as the flu virus. Some are abusers. You may be tempted to change them, but that's nearly impossible. The most difficult to avoid are "high voltage" people: you can't hold on and you can't let go. Break the current and move on. A cartoon sent from my late mother said: "Never try to teach a pig to sing. It wastes your time and it annoys the pig." Stay away from poi-sonous people. You are *not* responsible for them. Some family members are poisonous, so especially avoid them.

8. RENEW AND REENGAGE INSTEAD OF RETIRE. There comes a time for most of us when our job becomes tiresome or when we are less competent to do it. Get out at the top of your game. There is nothing more pathetic in the work-place than someone who stays too long. So get out. Then,

take time to recover from the grind of it. When you have, renew your commitment to something worthwhile, a new career or a cause or public service, an avocation, more time with the grandkids, reflection and meditation, reading the great books, developing a vibrant prayer life, rekindling an important relationship. Ask yourself, In fifteen years, what will I not be able to do? Make your bucket list, and then start crossing off those items. Remember that you will likely spend an extended time as a caregiver or care receiver. That may be a full-time job. So, prepare yourself for that eventuality and know where you can find help. Before then, share your life wholly with the ones you love, ones who have often had to settle for a fraction of your time and attention.

9. PLAN FOR ONE HUNDRED YEARS AND LIVE LIKE THERE'S NO TOMORROW. Howard Busby, a friend and Wesley Woods board member, is a financial-planning guru who introduced us to the magic of compound interest! Contrary to popular mythology, the government doesn't assure your life-style in retirement. Significant amounts of personal expense will likely be incurred for short- and long-term healthcare needs. Start saving money early and regularly. Get your legal house in order. It should be clear in writing who is authorized to make health decisions and manage your money in the event that you cannot. Discuss these decisions with family, a doctor, a lawyer, and a close friend or two. And get rid of as much stuff as you can except family history. As I heard a man say once, "You ain't never seen a U-Haul behind a hearse." Live like there's no tomorrow because one day there won't be. And don't leave your family with uncertainty or mess.

10. KEEP THE FAITH. People who maintain a religious life age more successfully than those who don't. Like our physical,

emotional, and social dimensions of life, the spiritual dimension changes as well. Learn to pray differently, more deeply, and more often. Prayer is the most and the least we can do for ourselves and anyone else. Meditation and reflective techniques can add deeper meaning to life. Worship, sharing life's struggles with kindred spirits, study, and service to others enhances health and engagement. Confession and reflection help with that ultimate conclusion as to whether or not life has been worthwhile.

11. GRIEVE WITHOUT REGRET. Many family members have told me one way or another, "When Mother dies, I want to look myself in the mirror and know I've done the best I could by her in the last years." Or, simply put, "No regrets." Grief without regret is cleansing. Regret carries the sicknesses that produces guilt and blame for many years and multiple generations. Woulda, coulda, shoulda can be deadly, while grieving the loss of someone we love can be freeing.

12. SAY GOOD-BYE. There comes a time for all of us to die. The issue for many is whether we say good-bye or avoid it, whether we ask forgiveness from those we have wronged or die with them resenting us for the rest of their own lives while there is still time to repair relationships. A disease like cancer gives us an immediate excuse to review our life, tell folks how much we love and appreciate them, get our affairs in order. A fatal heart attack doesn't. Dementia often doesn't because of the loss of memory and judgment. So, make every encounter a good-bye of sorts, and you will help yourself, your family, and your friends rest in peace. And at *every* gathering, *share stories!*

So, welcome to my *Hallowed Ground* stories. If you read this and at some future place, time, or situation you think of one of these stories, then this book has left its mark. Just as your story shared will do so for others. And remember, embedded in them are the secrets of successful aging.

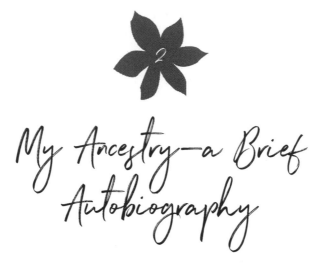

My Ancestry—a Brief Autobiography

"...inbreedin' don't work..."

As a small boy, I knew all four of my grandparents. I knew several couples who were Abraham and Sarah role models. I also observed the dark sides of aging and the poisonous people who created illness in the family that lasted through generations. I watched my parents carefully as they managed various family situations that confronted them as I grew up.

These elders and situations had a profound effect on me and my calling to the senior services field. My parents grew up in small mill and farm towns in rural Georgia. They were shaped by the hardships of the Depression and the sacrifices of World War II. One grandmother made clothes out of flour sacks while her husband raised and bartered food.

To more fully appreciate that background, a brief lesson in the southern language is in order. For example, when I refer to my aunt or uncle, I use "Ain" and "Unca." "Ma" and "Pa" are grandparent figures. "Lawd" refers to the Lord God Almighty, as in "Lawd, hep me," meaning, "Lord, I urgently require your assistance!" "Sho' nuff" is an affirmation of something someone just said: "Sure enough, I believe you." And rest assured that an expression of "Bless her heart" will follow any negative statement about an individual and justifies the previous harsh and judgmental opinion. For example, my late mother once told me a long-standing acquaintance was a "hu-er [southern for whore], bless her heart!"

Another southernism. I have family with lots of initial names: V.H., G.D., J.C., D.R. I had an Ain Way. Ain Babe. Snookie, Ain Girtie. Ain Aida Belle. Two generations of Unca Clarences. A Donna Sue. Johnnie Mae. Big Olivia. Little Olivia. Dootie. Dewey. Turk. Three sets of twins on my daddy's side: Bessie (my grandmother) and Jessie, Cora and Nora, and Ab and Ag (short for Abner and Agnes). And a cousin (married into the family) named "Frog." We also believe we have a relative who was a love child fathered by a late prominent political figure. I have a Cousin Bubba. And Snookie's claim to fame was that he drove the team bus for the minor league Atlanta Crackers. Sobriety was apparently not a criterion for minor league baseball team drivers, my late mother opined.

My ninety-two-year-old cousin Bubba is now my oldest living relative. He and his dearly departed wife, Rachel, were a modern Abraham and Sarah. For a generation, they took care of Rachel's sister, Patsy, who succumbed to polio over a many-year journey. Bubba and Rachel, along with their sons, Steve, Mickey, and David, were primary caregivers.

Bubba lives in Kennesaw, Georgia, just up the road. He was a *real* engineer, the kind that drove a train. He is bald, has one eye, and lives up to a law on the books in Kennesaw that requires citizens to own guns. He keeps two horses, and until a couple of years ago, he maintained a large garden, where he once grew an eighty-six-pound watermelon.

Bubba (real name Lamar) and Mother were like brother and sister. He was the oldest son of Mother's oldest sister, Ain Mae. Bubba and his family paid close attention to Mother, with frequent visits and invites to major family holiday events. Rachel and Mother were world-class country cooks. The New Year's Day feast at Rachel's included greens, black-eyed peas from the garden, butter beans, homemade chow-chow relish, hawg jowl (southern for hog jowls—a very fat part of a pig's face), meat loaf, cornbread, biscuits, homemade hot pepper sauce, corn, salmon patties, homemade sausage, and peach cobbler.

At one point, I challenged Mother and/or Rachel to write a southern cookbook entitled *1,001 Ways to Cook with Fatback*. After Daddy's second open-heart surgery that involved six bypasses, building on the five bypasses he had received a few years earlier, my mother lamented, "Well, I guess I'll have to change some of my recipes now that your daddy has this heart problem." No more fatback. Yet, when my mother died, I cleaned out her refrigerator and found five different kinds of sausage biscuits.

Bubba is like an older brother to me now. I call him regularly. More importantly, my daughter-in-law Elizabeth, David's wife, my toddler granddaughter, Lucinda, and I go to Kennesaw, pick up Bubba, and take him to one of his favorite country kitchen places on "all-you-can-eat chicken 'n' dumplings, fried chicken livers, or catfish day" specials for only eight bucks and change. Lucinda likes Bubba. He dotes on her; magical to watch.

Bubba adds to the family lore. On a long drive to visit Ain Jenny, he stunned me with this out-of-the-blue revelation: "Lawd, son. I'm gonna tell you somethin'. [Pause] Inbreedin' don't work. It don't work in huntin' dawgs. It don't work in horses. It don't work in cows. And it ain't worked in our family. And that's all I'm gonna say about that!" Family secrets passed on, yet mystery remaining. But Bubba, along with Cousin Marie, is my living conduit to the family jewels. Maintaining contact while we are all still alive will keep the family DNA viable.

My first personal hallowed-ground moment happened when I was three or four years old. I was standing in the gravel driveway of Ain Nettie and Unca Clarence's house, which was off a rural highway near Newnan, Georgia. My parents had dropped me off to go on a trip. They weren't very happy together. Daddy had returned from the war a different person from the fun-loving man Mother had married. Perhaps because of the emotional tension between my parents, I was happiest at Nettie and Clarence's house.

So, at age four or so, I was standing in that gravel driveway, crying, as my mother and daddy pulled away. With Ain Nettie and Marie standing there, Unca Clarence squatted down next to me. He had a heavy country drawl. And big, rough hands, with fingernails that rendered a screwdriver unnecessary. He was skinny, sinewy, a bag of sharp bones. Leathery skin and a wizened look that made him seem ancient to me, though he was only in his midthirties.

As I sniffled watching Mother and Daddy leave me, Unca Clarence reached around me from his squat, half hugged me, and, in a southern drawl, uttered what I was feeling, though I didn't have the words. "Way-ull [southern for 'well'], shiiiiiit!" (The longer you drag it out, the more effective and satisfying it is.)

I don't know that I had heard "shit" before, but I probably had. Instinctively, I knew it was expressive and naughty. Suddenly, my tears turned to a smile, then widened to a grin, as Unca Clarence hugged me. An old man in the family loved me. In fact, this was the first time in my life I was aware of feeling loved.

Nettie worked the day shift at the cotton mill, Clarence the night shift. Marie would babysit me while Clarence slept. When he woke up, we would do great things, like learn how to make "grub": baked beans with bacon. Or go fishing. Or burn the trash (no garbage pickup out in the country). Or paint the house. Or shoot birds with his .22 rifle. Or play checkers. Or draw horses on Unca Clarence's chalkboard while he sang "Wabash Cannonball."

Our family would spend Christmas at Nettie and Clarence's house. Santa Claus came down their chimney. The whole family, Mother and Nettie's side, which included all my grandmother Mama Roberts's children and grandchildren, would gather. Mama Roberts had nine kids and twenty-six grandchildren at her death in 1968. Clarence's kin were the Dinglers. I don't know how many of them there were, but Velma and Charlie lived one hundred yards down the path that included an open field for baseball or football, a field of rabbit tobacco, and a couple of outhouses. We were all blended cousins.

On Christmas Eve and Christmas Day, dozens of kin streamed in and out. It wasn't Christmas until you had been to Nettie and Clarence's house. Of course, we spent a few nights. Aunt Nettie rolled out pallets and sleeping bags. The house was cold at night. There were gas heaters in some of the rooms, but the possibility of fire prevented all of them from being lit at night. So we bundled up.

Being at Nettie and Clarence's was like being in the country home of God and his wife. (I believe He has one, though we won't delve into the theology of it.) When I eulogized Clarence, I told those gathered that being at that house in Newnan reminded me of the verse "In my Father's house are many rooms," where all are accepted and welcomed. Nothing fancy. A wooden framed house. Screened porch. A well that had to be monitored to keep the water level up.

By the time I was in *my* thirties, Clarence was truly an old man: even more leathery, wizened, and bony. He died of inhaling too much cotton fiber and smoking too many unfiltered Camels. Nettie was equally old, though she managed to keep her bottle of black hair dye handy. To me, they were another modern prototype of Abraham and Sarah—the biblical symbols of healthy aging—a role model for me who comes even more frequently to mind as I myself age.

When Unca Clarence died, I became acutely aware of my regret at not spending more time with him in his last years. It is painful to think of even now, as I turn seventy. I'm trying harder to keep up with Nettie and Clarence's daughter, my cousin Marie, who is the closest I have to an older sister. We talk frequently and visit rural cemeteries in search of ancestors, followed by another southern tradition: barbecue.

There were other elders in our family. Granddaddy Paul was my daddy's father. He bought me toys, gave me "frog skins" (dollar bills) that I could spend at the filling station on a Nehi Strawberry or Coca-Cola with Tom's salted peanuts poured into the top of the six-and-a-half-ounce Coke bottle. He was a supervisor at the cotton mill in Manchester, Georgia, and a kind and generous man. He and his wife, Bessie, did not get along. Once, Granddaddy Paul tried to stop her constant carping by telling her if she would just leave him alone, he would die as quickly as he could. He had not sought treatment for a heart condition and died days later. I was five, and his death left a big void in my life. He was only in his early fifties but seemed really old. I cherish his gold pocket watch, his platform rocker, and a bronze horse radio as remembrances.

My grandmother Bessie, whom I called Nana, was emotionally and sexually abusive to Daddy's two younger brothers, who lived tragic lives. She may have been evil, though in her local Methodist church she was regarded as a saint. She never approved of Mother, and after she heard that my parents had run away to get married, she sent them a black bedspread. Daddy could force himself to visit her only once a year, and even though she loved me, I could not bring myself to see her much more than that. My boys felt strange just being in her house, and I still have nightmares about a place that reminds me of her house in Manchester. Even on her deathbed, "Miss Bessie" refused pleas to reconcile with my mother and died saying she saw demons flying around her bed.

Paul and Nana's house was dark. They had separate bedrooms, with living and dining rooms pristinely kept, but with a lifeless feeling, tomblike. My boys called it "spooky" when they were young.

My grandmother came from the Dennis family. Ma Dennis was mean as a snake with a joyous countenance, like one of those beguiling, evil cartoon rats. I remember her sitting in the rocking chair, spitting her snuff residue into the fire with amazing accuracy. She could hit a number-ten empty tomato can six feet away. She brought up her daughters to abhor sex, prompting one son-in-law to return his bride (my grandmother Bessie's twin sister Jessie) and tell his mother-in-law she could keep her. As he left, the son-in-law pushed Ma Dennis into the fireplace. Ma Dennis had three sets of twins: Jessie and Bessie, Cora and Nora, and Abner and Agnes (Ab and Ag to us). Paul and Nana (a.k.a. Bessie) had separate bedrooms because Ma Dennis told her daughter to never have sex with her husband Paul again after the birth of their son, Paul Jr.

In spite of her personal meanness, Ma Dennis's children (with the exception of my grandmother) were sweet, gentle people, wonderful souls. Ag had a glass eye, no teeth, and always had a cold Coca-Cola and fresh coconut cake ready for us when we visited. Ab showed me how to whittle. He had a joyful chuckle like Santa Claus. George, born without a twin, was honored in a parade in his hometown of Palmetto, Georgia. Sitting in the back of a pickup truck, a sign read that he was "The Oldest Male in the County." "The Oldest Female" rode in her own pickup truck.

Unca George finally got too old to live at home and went into one of those mom-and-pop concrete block nursing homes along the highway. I visited him there one day, and he proudly informed me that he had a surprise for me. "Open the drawer to my dresser," he instructed. "I knew you were coming, and I've been saving you

my barbecue sandwich there for three days." I thanked him pro-
fusely and told him I would take it to my car right away to keep
someone else from getting it. There is probably no more lethal
ingestion in the South than a three-day-old unrefrigerated barbecue
sandwich. I used rubber gloves to dispose of it, but the gesture on
Unca George's part was memorable and touching.

I went into helping care for old people because of my experience with Mother's mother, Mama Roberts, who often lived with
us in our small house near Atlanta. Though sweet natured, she was
a lovable nuisance. She took over my room, so I slept on the couch.
Mother worked full-time. Daddy traveled. I was busy with school
activities and friends.

Mama Roberts was a disrupter in our lives, interrupting our
sleep by traipsing to the bathroom all night in her thick-heeled
old-lady shoes. Mother was responsible for most of her care, getting
up early to make her lunch, taking off time to take her to the
doctor. I knew the situation was hard on Mother, although she
loved her mother. It was only when I was an adult that she confided
to me and my wife, Kathleen, that she had become so depressed
during this time, she had all the knives removed from her house so
she wouldn't injure herself. Even though I didn't know things had
become that desperate for my mother, our experience as a family
helped me understand the pressures of caregivers I met during my
career.

When Mama Roberts was with us, I'd stop off at home from
school on my way to baseball or band practice. She would ask me
to take her to Woolworths for craft supplies or to the drugstore for
refills. Or she'd want me to watch *Divorce Court* with her on TV,
her favorite show. "Lawd, how people do!" she would exclaim as
wronged wives spun out their tales of betrayal. She had been alone
all day and just wanted company. She was so lonely she took to
calling strangers all around the country when direct dial became an
option, running up big phone bills for my parents.

Mama Roberts was a world-class tatter: a crafter of making lace out of string. She always had handkerchiefs for me to give to my teachers at Christmas or a pillowcase laced with tattin' for wedding gifts. She had long golden hair, which she brushed every morning before putting it in a braid that encircled her head. Yes, brushed golden hair strands were all over the house for weeks after her visits. It was like owning a golden retriever.

My grandfather, Papa Roberts, was a tenant farmer. After his death, Mama Roberts had no home of her own. She had initially lived in the old hotel in Greenville, Georgia, with Ain Sarah, who was widowed young, and Sarah's three kids. When that arrangement ended, Mama Robert's belongings were packed in a trunk, and she rotated living among four of her nine children. She spent a third of her time with us and the remainder with three of her other daughters, Nettie in Newnan, Jenny in Gainesville, and Mae in Greenville. She lived her last weeks with Mae and Doug in her beloved hometown of Greenville, Georgia.

One of the hardest parts of caregiving is the tension it can provoke between siblings. One of Mama Roberts's daughters, Olivia, lived on the next street over from ours. When Mama Roberts lived with us, Olivia rarely did anything for her, but she never hesitated to criticize my mother. One day the dynamics came to a head, with Olivia calling Mama Roberts while Mother was at work. Olivia apparently asked how she was doing with an undertone, I suspect, of suspicion about how well she was being treated in our family. She asked Mama Roberts if she had adequate food. When Mother got home from work, Olivia unloaded on her, ending, "And all you left her for lunch was dill pickles and chocolate ice cream!"

Mother was furious. I now think that Olivia was bipolar and self-medicated with alcohol. She was a mean drunk. A family war erupted, with wounds that lasted for years after Mama Roberts had died. There was some reconciliation after Olivia had a stroke, and after her daughter, Little Olivia, died from cancer. Yet, I don't believe Mother ever forgave Olivia for her neglect of Mama Roberts. The Bible says God forgives, when asked, and then forgets. When it comes to caregiver tensions, some families can do neither. The dynamics are visited on future generations.

My father, who liked few people, had reverence for Mama Roberts. I never heard him complain about her crowding into our tiny house. Daddy was an Archie Bunker personality (if you are old enough to remember the television show *All in the Family*): rigid, cynical, prejudiced, and yet fair and just and loving in his own limited way. Daddy was a man of few words, but it was not wise to ask him his opinion of your situation if you didn't want to hear it. One day, sitting in the carport with Daddy drinking a glass of Mother's wonderful sweet tea, I was whining about some predicament I found myself in, partially of my own making. Daddy listened, took a puff of his Tampa Nugget, and said, "Life is like walking through a cow pasture, son. About every third step is a pile of shit. Get used to it."

Daddy served in the army in World War II. He was stationed in England, helping prepare for the Normandy invasion. His convoy to England survived storms and German submarines; in England there were bombings. He said it was enough to make grown men cry. His advice to those in hysterics was harsh, but effective: "Go see the chaplain, get your 'tough shit' card punched, and get back to work."

My father convinced me that success and satisfaction in life come from learning to deal successfully with shit. We all face it. How do we deal with it? Leadership guru Warren Bennis says that great leaders are forged in the crucible of adversity. Others have said we learn more from failure than success, more from tough times than good times. We remember—and hopefully savor—the good times. But we learn from the tough ones. This is why I believe the hard times we go through with our own elderly loved ones can be transformed into peace of mind with no regrets.

Daddy and I were never really close. In my early years, he was a traveling salesman. He came home Friday night and left Sunday afternoon. Because of Daddy's job, we moved around until I was nine, when we bought a home in a new post–World War II subdivision called Belvedere, near Decatur, Georgia.

I have no memories of Daddy until I was four or five. He and Mother rarely seemed happy together. She admitted as much after he died. "We were married for sixty-two years!" she remembered. "It was only the last twenty-six that we were miserable." She didn't realize what she had said.

Daddy played a behind-the-scenes role in our lives. Though our family helped to found the Belvedere United Methodist Church, Daddy got to church early to make the coffee and stayed late to count the offering. He couldn't sit through most services; he was too restless. He rarely went to my Little League games but helped prepare our first Little League field. He bought me a trumpet, but it was like pulling teeth to get him to attend a band concert. I never heard "I love you" from him, and he only told me once he was proud of me, and that was prompted by Kathleen on the occasion of graduation with my doctorate degree. Daddy was largely unavailable emotionally. Yet, on his deathbed, he and I filled an emotional hole in eight hours that had taken a lifetime to dig. I speak of it in chapter 8, "Dying and Death."

With our two boys, John and David, Daddy displayed a different dimension of himself. What he lacked in fathering, he made up for in grandfathering. He even quit smoking his beloved Tampa Nuggets because the boys were allergic to the smoke. John named Daddy "Da" at a very early age. And he labeled Mother "Mamie." Mamie and Da, they will forever be known. These names are on their tombstones in Greenville. What little joy Mamie and Da shared with each other was generated around their roles as grandparents. Our boys loved them dearly.

More about the family history. The year after Mama Roberts

died was the most important year of my life. In 1969 I was fixed up with a blind date. Her name was Kathleen Wright, a sophomore transfer student to Emory University, where I was a senior. I was on the rebound from an earlier relationship, and the breakup had come close to the Sigma Chi formal. Kathleen was a newly minted Tri Delta pledge.

A bit of the mystical occurred. As she was about to come to the lobby of her dorm to meet me, she stopped by the room of her big sister in the sorority, where several other sisters were sitting around chatting. Someone asked where she was going. She said she had a blind date with a guy named Larry Minnix. A sorority sister said, "Oh, he's a loser!" Whereupon Kathleen said, "Now, don't make fun of him. I'll probably wind up marrying him!" And so it was by the end of the year!

I was immediately attracted to her. She glowed with personality. She was very interesting and pretty; still so today. And she had a sense of humor and thought I was funny. And she was deeply spiritual. I was twenty-one, Kathleen nineteen. I fell in love with her *instantly*. We were both students—I was in theology school by then—and probably too young to get married. It seemed like the thing to do at the time, however. We had little money, classes by day, and me working at the mental hospital evenings and nights. After she graduated from Emory, Kathleen worked in a personnel office while I finished my doctorate, helping put me through theology school. Then I returned the favor, putting her through graduate school at Georgia State University.

Our parents helped financially. Mine fed us Sunday lunch with plenty of leftovers to take home and handed out twenty-dollar bills for dinner and a movie. Hers gave us their old car, invited us to accompany them to Mexico and Europe, and presented us with the down payment on our first house. We have tried to keep alive this tradition of generosity of both sets of parents with our own children.

Sunday lunch at Mamie and Da's included three meats from a repertoire of meat loaf, pot roast, BBQ ribs, fried chicken, salmon patties, and country-fried steak, accompanied by deviled eggs and half a dozen vegetables flavored with fatback. There was cornbread, though Mama lamented to the day she died, "Lawd, my cornbread is no good. It just falls apart." Pecan pie or cobbler was always the closer.

My family was uneasy with Kathleen. She was well educated, aspiring to complete a PhD. Though her parents came up the hard way during the Depression and World War II, Mother thought I was marrying into a level of society where I might not fit. I believe her parents felt the same way for a while. We married at Glenn Memorial Church on the campus of Emory University, in part because Kathleen wanted to avoid the socialite spotlight wedding that would occur in Dallas, Texas, where she grew up, and in part because her parents had married at the Glenn Church in the middle of World War II, shortly before her father shipped out to Europe.

To highlight the tension caused by our different backgrounds, Kathleen went into a panic when my father told her, without cracking a smile, that my side of the family would show up at the wedding in church buses, spread picnic blankets on the beautiful grounds of Glenn Memorial Church, which served as the grand structure and welcomed the public to the Emory Campus, and nurse their babies out in the open.

The first few years together, Kathleen and I worked the kinks out of our relationship. Several years were pretty tough, but we never wanted to divorce—at least not at the same time. We had our first pet, a Siamese cat named Boo, and for a while, the only thing that kept us together was that neither one of us wanted to give up custody of Boo. Thanks to God and therapy, and because we were always best friends, we got through the worst of it.

One time she got mad at me. She happened to be taking a graduate seminar in Freudian psychology, and she exclaimed to me,

"Honestly, you're the only person I know who is hung up in every phase of life development!" Initially I felt complimented. I said to myself, "I'm an omnitalented, well-balanced Renaissance man." Then I realized what she meant: I was stuck in all Freud's phases of life development—oral, anal, and genital!

My family was intimidating to Kathleen. She was never comfortable around them in the early years. She was private; they were open about everything. She was a loner; they were huggers. She enjoyed intellectual pursuits; they liked ribald humor. Kathleen thought the mark of a successful woman was professional achievement, and my family expected women to cook and clean and have babies. In fact, Mother had a high chair stationed in the kitchen when we returned from our honeymoon.

One of my cousins, Johnnie Mae, could be particularly catty in her queries about our plans for children. Every time we met, she would begin with, "Let's see, Kathleen, you and Larry don't have any children yet, do you?" Kathleen asked my advice about how to respond to Johnnie Mae. I told her to think of a humorous quip with an edge to it. So, at the next family reunion, Johnnie Mae began, "Let's see, Kathleen, you and Larry don't have any children yet, do you?" Whereupon Kathleen retorted, "No, Johnnie Mae, not yet. Larry just can't get it up."

The room erupted. Kathleen passed some test in the eyes of the family. The inquiry never happened again, but when the boys were born, John in 1978 and David in 1982, Johnnie Mae scrutinized them carefully for family resemblance.

As we raised our children and added to our family of animals, I rose in the ranks at Wesley Woods, and Kathleen completed her PhD and wrote an award-winning biography of the nineteenth-century evangelist Sam Jones, entitled *Laughter in the Amen Corner*. He was a colorful character, a reformed alcoholic, and likely bipolar. At one time, he was the most quoted man in America. She began teaching college history and loved it.

We had a great life, but we had too much going on, which created stress. My folks lived nearby and were enormously helpful to us with babysitting. Mother and Daddy's home was happy when the boys were there, unhappy when they were not. But Mother and Daddy began to have health problems, especially Daddy, with light strokes and heart problems.

We would travel to Texas once or twice a year, and Mr. and Mrs. Wright always welcomed us. Christmastime, Kathleen's brother, Larry, and sister, Rosalind, would bring their spouses and children from Boston and Austin, and all the kids would sleep on pallets in the living room, much as I had at Nettie and Clarence's house. Mr. Wright always arranged tickets to the Cotton Bowl or a Dallas Cowboys game.

As our parents aged, life got more complicated. Daddy's heart disease and difficult personality had to be managed. I had to watch carefully for any signs of physical abuse of my mother. I had to tell him at one flash point that I'd put him in one of my nursing homes if he ever laid a hand on her. He said he'd starve himself to death if I did. I said, "Your choice. So be it! But that's exactly what I'll do." He never hit her, and I never had to follow through with my threat.

A lesson here on promises you may not be able to keep. Never promise you won't put an elder in a nursing home! Sometimes, that is the only safe place for them to live.

Kathleen's caregiving responsibilities increased and were long distance. Caregiving will test the strength of a marriage. Her faithfulness to her parents and mine increased my admiration for her. However, these years sapped time and energy from her professional pursuits, while my career soared. She gave up a lot for our families. And she did so while managing a chronic illness, diagnosed when she was in her early thirties. In Kathleen's case, there is a gene pool that contains grit and an autoimmune disorder, obviously opponents in the overall health of a person like her. Grit is winning, but at a price.

Our boys have done well. They both have their own businesses. John married Laura, and they have Elise, now four, and twin boys Sam and Will, who are one year old. David married Elizabeth, and they are parents of Lucinda, age two, and are expecting a new daughter. Our daughters-in-law are sources of joy and pride for us, and we delight in our grandchildren, who have made ours a good old age.

Reflecting on my own history, Nettie and Clarence were the matriarch and patriarch, the Abraham and Sarah of my family. Bubba and Rachel were prototypes as well. Mama Roberts's situation represents the underlying dynamics that families face in caregiving, especially when a senior is passed around from house to house. There were skeletons in the Dennis and Minnix branches of the family. Exposing them helped us break the cycle of addiction and abuse.

Kathleen and I had persevered, as had our parents. No victims or deniers. We also found the humor in our situations, filled with the pathos produced by flawed characters and inherited circumstances. In fact, I borrowed perseverance from her. She had plenty to share.

So far there are no storybook endings, but there is a measure of redemption for everyone, and many lessons to be learned about the secrets of successful aging: the importance of family heritage, including skeletons, the need to tend loved ones, and the impact poisonous people can have down through the generations, the humor to be found, and the predisposition to heart disease and addiction. But most importantly, the character choice to *persevere.*

All were hallowed-ground experiences for me. All helped me find my calling. I hope some of you can identify.

I have come to strongly believe what the Book of Romans says about the importance of perseverance: "Perseverance produces character; character produces hope; and hope never disappoints us," which gets me to the importance of attitude. Attitude is understood and shaped by knowing your ancestry.

Attitude: Personal Faith Perspective

"...dog food or mystery..."

I talk about the secret of attitude in three parts. This chapter is on our personal attitude about growing old. The next is on society's attitude. The third is on the characteristics of older people who have a healthy attitude about it.

Early in my career as the administrator of Wesley Woods, I came to know Mr. Hohaus and Mr. Miller, two residents. I was in theology school at Emory in the early 1970s and was asked to bring a couple of residents to a class so my fellow students could gain insight into the residents' perspective about their own aging. I asked Hohaus and Miller: "So, what's it like to grow old?"

Miller, in his late eighties, said, "Life at my age is meaningless. I don't know why I've lived this long, but I don't have the guts to take my own life. So, maybe I'll die soon and they can make dog food out of me." A nervous titter went through the classroom. Miller himself was chuckling as he spoke, but there was no question he was serious.

Hohaus countered, "You know, Miller, I see it differently. I'm ninety-two. I've lived through the horse and buggy to the space age and two world wars. I've lost kids and even grandkids. I've understood little of the mysteries of all this, but I've made it to ninety-two. So, I go to bed at night and make sure I'm not out of sorts with anybody I love. And if I don't wake up, it's OK; just another mystery I will get through."

Two very different perspectives on aging and dying, based on very different personal attitudes about life, faith, and personal beliefs.

I would guess we would all like to age and face death with Hohaus's confidence. We all know of people like him. They seem to have a calm about them. Life is a means, a passage to some greater state. Every stage of life has its gains and losses, its triumphs and tragedies, its transformations and inevitabilities, dreams and disappointments. This attitude is based on the belief that life has been good and the next mysterious phase will be even better.

Let's see what a preschooler has to offer in terms of attitudes about aging. The Reverend Woody Spackman, now retired from the position of director of pastoral services for Emory Healthcare, told the story of a chaplain intern at Wesley Woods who also had a part-time position in a church, directing the children's program. In her project of interviewing young kids, she asked a group of them a question: "What does God think of old people?" A little girl immediately responded, "He likes them. They need God. And they know it. And God is grateful for that."

Based on this child's perspective, I have arrived at a definition of aging and fulfillment. I define aging through a theological lens as the process of living through which God reminds us of our dependence on a power beyond ourselves. And fulfillment as we age is a state of reconciliation with God, people we care most about, and ourselves, so that we conclude that life has been worthwhile. Hohaus verbalized these definitions. What does fulfillment sound like?

My good friend John Diffey, now retired after a distinguished career in senior living with the Kendall organization, told me of the older woman who simply walked into his office one day and declared, "I've concluded that I'm OK with the universe, Johnny boy! How about you?"

That little girl who thought God likes old people had it right, but where did she acquire that perspective? I am sure Miller and Hohaus's views were shaped early. I know Miller's was reinforced in his professional life. He was a troubleshooter for a railroad company. He saw problems everywhere. His perspective, I'm convinced, was that life is a series of never-ending problems. He lived out the rest of his life miserably, alienating staff in the senior community where he lived and his family, who no doubt longed for his death to put him and them out of their misery.

Life can deal cruel blows that can either leave us bitter or more confident. I watched my wife Kathleen inform her bedbound father of the unexpected death of his wife, her mother. A hard conversation. Many years of marriage. A bootstraps, self-made man married to a southern belle. They fell in love just before he left for combat in Europe under General Patton. They were "an item" in today's vernacular.

Kathleen grabbed his hand, clutched it, and talked straight to him. "Daddy, Mother has died suddenly. Her heart stopped, and they couldn't revive her at the emergency room. Daddy, you have a choice. You can give up and die soon yourself. Or you can get through this and enjoy the time with your family you have left. I hope you'll stay with us." She was instinctive about how to handle the situation. How did she come by that?

He did stay for another thirteen months. He had disabilities from strokes, but he enjoyed visits with family, rides to see the sights, and even a couple of weekend trips to nearby resorts.

None of it was easy. But when he died, among his last words were "Glorious, glorious, glorious!" as he saw things we couldn't see. And Kathleen knew she had done the best she could.

Kathleen offered him a choice about his perspective. Faith shapes life and the living. Yet faith is itself tested by life. Note that I did not say God tests us. Life does. Blaming God for life events leads people down a blind alley of a bitter faith. Hoyt Oliver, among the very best teachers I ever had, is a professor emeritus at Oxford College of Emory University. Hoyt had a major crisis of faith. His sister, who was mentally ill, wandered away from the institution where she lived, in the dead of winter, and froze to death. Hoyt turned to alcohol with angry outbursts to family, friends, and God, whom he blamed for his sister's death. God caused it, he raved.

Hoyt assumed a cruel and angry God who randomly selected people to die to teach some kind of mysterious lesson to survivors, or, in the case of the death of children, because God needed a new flock of angels in heaven. These are not uncommon perceptions of the power and motivation of God even today. They have enormous influence on human behavior...Hoyt's in particular.

Then, as Hoyt journeyed through an alcohol recovery program, in the midst of a rave about and to God, he said a message came to him. A clear message. Not an audible voice, not a hallucination, but a clear, calm message, and it was this: "I did not take your sister. I received her."

A clear turning point in Hoyt's recovery. A change in his faith perspective.

Further perspective on theological perceptions that influence lives is in the story of Mary B. Jordan. She was an African American business entrepreneur in Atlanta at a time when there were two sides of the tracks in the emerging Civil Rights era of the 1950s and 1960s. Mary Jordan was a great cook, which became known. She started what became Atlanta's premier catering service, Mary B.

Jordan Catering. "Not a prominent Atlanta wedding or bar mitzvah that she didn't handle," one Atlantan told me.

Mary B. Jordan had three sons, one of whom is the well-known Vernon Jordan, one of America's distinguished citizens in business, politics, civil rights, and philanthropy. I came to know Vernon as Mrs. Jordan's son. She had a severe stroke and had to live her final years at Wesley Woods. Vernon attended care conferences, traveling from Washington, DC. He called me frequently about his mother, asking me to deliver messages to her. Her eyes would widen, and she would manage a slight grin in her impaired state at the mention of Vernon's name.

Vernon lived Atlanta civil rights history, challenges, and transformation. He wrote an outstanding book about it called *Vernon Can Read!* Vernon's mother saw that he went to college, wrote to him every day, admonished him to pray, and set aside a dime of every dollar for his future and another dime to give to "the Lawd."

Mary B. Jordan was a great woman in many ways. But her theological perspective was life-changing for Vernon. Vernon's reputation as a civil rights leader was on a meteoric rise, as was that of his first wife, Shirley. A dynamic couple—until she developed multiple sclerosis. At the time, there were few effective treatments. He foresaw tough consequences personally and professionally for both his wife and himself.

So, Vernon sought his mother's counsel. He said he laid out the story and his fears for their future. His mother listened. When he got his lamentations out of his system, Mary B. Jordan responded simply. As he wrote in his book *Vernon Can Read!*:

"Why did this happen to Shirley?…Why did this happen to me?"

She said, "Son, the Lord doesn't give you more of a load than you can tote. That's your load. Now tote it. Is there anything else you want to talk about?"

"No, ma'am." There was nothing more to be said: "That's your load, now tote it." I was still sad…but my mother's words stiffened my spine and resolve…I knew we would have to…make a new future with the particular hand that life had dealt us. (p. 188)

So, where does a Hohaus, Miller, or Mary Jordan attitude come from? Are we born with it? Or does it evolve with our life experiences as they knock us around? How did a preschooler so confidently express her belief about God's attitude toward old people, and more deeply, how ultimately dependent are we on a creative power far beyond our mortality?

How did Kathleen so quickly and intuitively know how to handle her father's situation on the death of her mother? How did she know that his reaction to the event was a matter of choice?

How did Hoyt come by the notion that God caused his sister's death to teach some kind of lesson? Yet, how was he open enough to receive an inaudible but clear message that he was looking at the situation in the wrong way?

How did Mary Jordan know that God will help us "tote" it? Wherever does our personal theological perspective come from?

How do we explore it as life tests us? Are we open to changing it by listening for messages of divine guidance? How do we accept the mysterious, explore its unknown, through whatever means at our disposal? How do we continue to cultivate a relationship with God, by whatever label we place on the divine?

Whatever our answers are to these questions, they create the fundamental perspective that defines our attitude about old people and growing old. And if that attitude is Milleresque, we have much psychological and spiritual work to do. Otherwise, we will face the end of our lives with despair instead of integrity, as Erikson described our last late-life conflict to be resolved.

Further, the Miller perspective creates generations of problems for caregivers. In the midst of aging, disability, stresses, and shared caregiving, it is easy to lament, "How long, O Lord, how long?" There is usually plenty of blame to go around: family who disappoint, fight among themselves; bad choices; diseases; treatments that don't work; accidents; and a God who allowed this mess to happen and won't magically solve it for us, a God who might seem to let some people linger and suffer and others die too soon for reasons we can't fathom. While God has broad shoulders and can take our blaming, ultimately people who age successfully and die at a good old age come to the conviction that God doesn't cause problems with which we must cope. Rather, God gave the possibility of new life, with all its difficulties and opportunities that he helps us get through. Without that fundamental attitude of faith in the mystery, life can become bitter and depressing for all involved.

So, in dealing with the universal phenomenon called aging, we can wonder why and curse the darkness—or accept the reality and ask for help, pray for meaning and strength. We can make dog food of life or live the mystery. A choice of perspective about life and faith in a higher power that will help us tote it all.

So, where does society's attitude about aging and old people come from?

Attitude: Societal Perspective

"...organ recital or engaging personality..."

I found myself in an East Coast airport, flying west. I wound up walking next to an elderly couple and could overhear talk about a new great-great-granddaughter just born in Oregon. The husband accompanied his wife to the gate. She and I were the first passengers to arrive there. We struck up a conversation. Yes, she was on the way to help her great-granddaughter take care of a new baby. She proudly reported her age as eighty-eight.

A gate attendant arrived. He offered us a cup of coffee (back in the day!), but he related to us differently. To me, he was matter-of-fact, with a conversational tone. To her, he spoke more slowly and raised his voice as if she were deaf. As boarding time approached, another attendant approached the woman again to see if she needed a wheelchair down the ramp and wondered if she would prefer a seat near the lavatory. She declined both.

However, there was an increasingly skeptical lilt in her voice. She leaned over to me and asked if I thought she should use the wheelchair and sit near the toilet. I looked at her and said, "Lady, I watched you walk half a mile to get to this gate. You must have some measure of strength and ability to be traveling across country to help your great-granddaughter with her newborn. Don't let these nice people turn you into some kind of invalid. I'm betting you can walk and go to the bathroom by yourself."

The great-great-grandmother encountered an attitude all too common in society about older people: that aging is equivalent to disease and decline, which affect self-confidence. Based on that attitude, we begin to treat older people accordingly: a self-fulfilling prophecy develops.

So, where does the disease and decline syndrome come from? We can turn to anthropology for an answer. The first book I read when I entered the field of aging was the Pulitzer Prize–winning effort by Simone de Beauvoir called *The Coming of Age.* She studied the attitudes and practices of ancient and current, sophisticated and primitive societies about older people and aging. She concluded that few societies throughout written culture and history have dealt fairly with their elders; that, in fact, it was inherent in the human species to push our elders aside when they become useless and needy to make way for the next generation.

De Beauvoir cited modern societies that relegate their older women to a place in the corner to be fed with scraps from the table. One had a ceremony where the older man is clubbed to death by his family to get him out of the way. She says the modern equivalent is the limited pensions provided to older women today: scraps from society's table, along with the "gold watch" syndrome where older men are forced into retirement based on arbitrary age. De Beauvoir historically cites the Romans at their height of political control and the Chinese as the only major societies that treated their elders in respectful ways.

Robert Butler, MD, and Myrna Lewis, MSW, wrote a classic

book entitled *Aging and Mental Health* back in the 1970s, where they outline myths about aging, such as that older people are senile or unproductive or that they lose curiosity and creativity, becoming disinterested and disengaged.

A dominant theory about aging when I entered the field was "peak-decline." Birthday traditions of "over the hill" parties are a prominent symbol of this theory. Attendant to "peak-decline" was "disengagement theory." That is, older people naturally want to withdraw from society, a la the mythical elder Eskimo that is put on the ice floe, never to be seen again. This idea resulted in the proliferation of institutions for seniors and the slow growth of services that support elders at home and programs that facilitate staying engaged in life and community.

There are people with conditions that cannot be managed responsibly at home anymore, as some of my stories already highlight. But society has too much invested in having all of us believe that we become an accumulation of our diseases and disabilities instead of an accumulation of our unique experiences, relationships, insights, and creativity.

Dr. Bill Thomas, author of *What Are Old People For?* offers another perspective. He assumes that nature has a purpose for everything and notes that in most animal species, critters die right after their usefulness is depleted. When females cannot reproduce or when males can no longer protect and provide, demise follows soon thereafter.

However, Thomas has a very different take on the use and strength of older women in the human species. Far from the common view that the gate attendant reflected, that older women are weak and dependent, Thomas notes that women outlive men. But why? He says it is because grandmothers have a pivotal role in advancing the human species because they help raise children while mothers and fathers protect, defend, and provide for the family unit. In fact, Thomas suggests that humans dominate the planet because older women have assured the survival of our young. A far cry from peak decline as we age.

My wife and I took a cruise several years ago. Adjacent to our breakfast table group was a larger table of what appeared to be five generations of a family; I'll call them the Waltons. I noticed that individual members began to peel away from the table, and I overheard part of a conversation. What appeared to be a young adult grandson, "John Boy," approached Grandma Walton and asked how she was doing. Her immediate response was, "Well, the sores on my leg are not festering nearly as badly today as they were yesterday."

Too late for John Boy to peel off. Others began to abandon the table like rats on a sinking ship. He was stuck. I thought of how many other ways Grandma Walton *could* have responded: "The entertainment last night was lovely" or "I had an interesting conversation with two of my great-grands" or "I read up on the excursions for the day and want to hear all about your adventures when you come back to the boat." Lots of options other than the state of her festering sores. Attitude. She had become her diseases. Society enabled that to occur over generations of attitudes.

A dear family friend, Harold, dropped by my parents' house one hot Saturday while I was there. Harold's wife, Dot, was dying of cancer. A family member had given Harold some relief, so he came to see Mother and Daddy. I asked him why our house if he had some free time. He replied, "I need a few laughs. Your mother and daddy always have something to laugh about. People visit us, but all I get to hear is their organ recitals; they talk about their livers, their intestines, their heart problems. I don't want to hear any of that. I want a few laughs."

Too many of us as we age respond to how we're doing with organ recitals. Society taught us that language. Then we wonder why no one calls or visits anymore. After my father had his second set of bypass surgeries, my mother became consumed with his bodily functions and the fear that he could have another heart episode, which was inevitable, given his health. The two of them were stewing in their own juice at home, mad at each other, twenty-four seven. So, I took a day off and told Mother I'd drive her "down to the country"—which was code for her beloved hometown of Greenville, Georgia. We'd see relatives, visit the cemetery, have several hours in the car to talk, review family history and lore. Forty-five minutes into the trip, all Mother had talked about was the frequency, quantity, and color of Daddy's intake and output. A moment of truth in our relationship: Do I just listen? Or do I get her on another, more appealing track?

I took a risk. I said, "Mother, ya know, all you have talked about since you got in the car is Daddy's urine and feces and how many bites of peas he ate for dinner. If that's the nature of your conversation with your friends and our kinfolks, you'll find people not wanting to talk with you pretty soon. No one wants to hear that. Besides, you are a much more interesting person than that."

Then, a classic guilt-inducing response, followed by a realization. "You ought to be ashamed of yourself, talking to your mother like that...But I guess you're right." Behind her talk about his current condition was her anxiety about it. She was even afraid to leave him for the day for fear he'd die. I was blunt: the next episode would probably bring death whether she was there or not. And I bet her that he was glad to have some peace and quiet without her. She paused but changed her tune the rest of the trip. When we returned home, he was still alive. Hard to tell if she was relieved or disappointed.

I remember when I personally experienced ageism. It was on the occasion of my annual physical just after I turned sixty-five. My physician, an internist and geriatrician at a prestigious academic medical center, had an entourage of a geriatric fellow, a medical resident, and a student. She asked if it was OK with me if the

35

fellow conducted certain tasks of the physical exam. I, of course, agreed.

The young doctor engaged me by stating in a louder, slower voice (much like the eighty-eight-year-old great-grandmother experienced from the airport gate attendant), "Mr. Minnix, since you are now sixty-five, there are certain things we do for people your age. Is that OK?" I looked at him and responded slowly and more loudly, "It's OK as long as it doesn't involve rubber gloves and KY jelly." I noticed a muffled chortle from my doctor as a non-plussed countenance formed around the face of the fellow. In any event, I avoided a prostate exam that day. I've often wondered if my doctor helped him reflect on his attitude and approach.

Perhaps among all sectors of American society, ageism is most prominent in the health and services delivery system. This is ironic, given the fact that our country spends more money on aging geriatric healthcare than any other developed economy. We overtreat some seniors and underserve others. Dr. Atul Gwande of Harvard is a modern guru on how American attitudes about aging are reflected in care delivery design. His provocative article in *The New Yorker* magazine a few years ago identified communities and individuals on whom millions have been spent inappropriately. His subsequent books and studies provide further evidence of inappropriate resource application based on systemic health delivery.

Here's how these systemic issues play out in real-life situations. My late father-in-law experienced multiple strokes over a period of time. On one occasion, he was sent by ambulance to a comprehensive, prestigious medical center where his primary care physician practiced. His live-in caregiver had instructions on his personal desire to be offered an effective medication that dissolved clots quickly to minimize permanent stroke damage. He lay on a gurney in the hospital ER hallway for hours, in spite of pleas by his caregiver and children (by phone) to administer the medication. Family was even told that he was receiving the drug, which never occurred. He later reflected that he felt like a "sack of potatoes" on the gurney, with no one relating to him in the middle of his crisis.

In another example, an African American elder was referred to Wesley Woods by her church friends. She had been in and out of a large hospital multiple times in recent weeks, only to be sent home when Medicare coverage ended for each episode of illness, but her friends noticed her continued steady decline. Wesley Woods employed geriatricians and geriatric-trained nurses, two of whom went to her home and reported that she had rehabilitation potential "if the bedsore the size of a pie in the middle of her back didn't kill her first." (Which, by the way, it did!) She was a multiple admission and discharge patient at a large hospital whose staff did not notice a pressure ulcer the size of a pie.

A resource-rich university community with a generous public transportation budget kept noticing that senior transportation topped the list of connect needs in their community. This was puzzling until an analysis that showed that their handicapped vehicles were largely deployed to student-convenient locations instead of senior or disability communities—a huge mismatch of need with ample resources.

A woman from a low-income community-home setting was referred to Wesley Woods through Georgia's Medicaid program. She was mildly impaired and homebound. Her medical care was rendered by various clinics based in an inner-city hospital. It was thought that she needed to be in a nursing home. Our medical evaluation found that part of her impairment was due to medication mismanagement. She was on fifty-two medicines, including twelve inhalers for asthma! Of course, physician and clinic labels were on each bottle. She became better managed and remained at home.

In my Washington responsibilities, cabinet secretaries, members of Congress who chair various healthcare committees, and White House officials have asked me a variety of questions that one way or another boil down to this: what one or two things could policymakers do to improve quality of care for seniors and save taxpayer money? My responses: require every medical student to take a course in geriatric pharmacology in order to recognize chemical mismanagement and invest in more outreach and low-income subsidized senior housing with basic services-coordination capabilities. Today we have a generous senior drug benefit and no requirement that doctors are trained to prescribe the drugs. Low-income housing for seniors continues to shrink.

Lest it be assumed that the health system issues just impact poor seniors, my dear friend Jerry Eickhoff called me to describe his father's situation. Ike, as his father was called, had been forced to retire by his company. He was a traveling salesman and was precipitously given the gold-watch treatment. Ike had not done well at home: conflict with his wife, lack of motivation, lethargy.

Jerry had paid out of pocket for Ike to be evaluated at more than one medical center, with the fear that Ike had developed cancer. But no test results could find any sign of it. Jerry asked if our Wesley Woods geriatrician could evaluate Ike further. I told Jerry I believed his dad was clinically depressed and needed to see a geriatric psychiatrist. "What!" he said. "I could never get my old man to see a shrink."

I told Jerry I thought I could. We set an appointment. Ike told me his saga and revealed that he believed he might be dying of cancer but the family didn't want to tell him.

I said to him, "Ike, I have another theory, and I bet I'm right. I think you are clinically depressed and need to see a psychiatrist. Not one of those you see on TV that has a beard and asks you why you hated your mother. No, these are shrinks that use medicine and talk therapy to help you get through the big change of retirement."

"OK, if you think it will help, I'll do it." He did and got better. Jerry recalled that Ike loved to paint in his younger days and supplemented therapy with art lessons. Ike became a prolific artist.

Over time, though, Ike developed a small thyroid tumor that

had to be removed. The recovery produced a stroke. But with care coordination from a geriatrician and continued psychiatric outpatient support, Ike learned painting techniques that compensated in part for stroke damage. He produced a new genre of his own art, and he lived several years as a beloved member of the family through numerous difficulties. The two prime ingredients to the "load" that Ike and his family had to "tote" admirably were access to the right medical care for Ike's changing situation and family support.

Ageism is alive and well in our society, even in our resource-rich medical system. It is based on a fear of growing old and dying and outdated care and service models. Too many comedic images of older people like Tim Conway's doddering, shuffling old character, and not enough recognition of men like Picasso or Ronald Reagan. Too many Jonathan Winters's Maude Frickert, and not enough showcasing of Betty White or GE's Millie Dresselhaus in their commercials to promote women in the engineering arenas. The stereotypes linger in religious denominations slow to recognize the equality and importance of women clergy. Male clergy leaders still hide behind long-standing, man-produced doctrines and hierarchies that say that women are subservient.

Somewhere between de Beauvoir's study on the pervasiveness of ageism historically and Thomas's recognition that older women are the stronger sex, there is progress on societal attitudes about older people and aging. In the meantime, we must fight the peak-decline perception and disengagement theory and mismanagement, which have led us to ill personal and societal health.

Attitude: Exemplars

"...the smoldering embers..."

So, what does a healthy attitude about growing old look like when you see one? Let me introduce you to older people I have encountered: characters to help you discern the characteristics that make them exemplars of successful aging. The first is a man I encountered in the San Antonio airport.

As I battled the foot traffic to my gate, I noticed an approaching individual who was parting the crowds. I'd guess he was over eighty years old. Tanned, sinewy, leathery skin. Silver-haired flattop. He moved with a bold determination, with a fixed stare as if on a mission to whip someone at the local bar. He wore short, anatomically correct athletic pants, white tennis shoes, black socks. He sported a T-shirt that read, "The smoldering embers of a fiery youth!" Attitude personified! I'd say that his attitude about himself at his age was still fueled by *passion*. Successful aging never loses a passion for family, friends, causes, and creativity. We can still be alive and lively at any age if we maintain *passion*.

The second is Virginia, a spark plug, an impish woman who began to decline physically, necessitating a move from Wesley Woods independent living to the nursing home. Linda Rosen, one of the world's great social workers and dear friend of Virginia, helped her make the hard transition. Linda, in her deeply empathetic way, commented to Virginia how difficult this change must be for her. Virginia looked her in the eye, grinned, and quipped, "Yes, but I've decided to get up every morning, tuck my titties in my pantyhose, and keep on walkin'!" I'd say that Virginia reflects a characteristic I'd call *perseverance*. Notice she "has decided." Yes, attitude is a choice. If *passion* is the fuel of a healthy attitude, *perseverance* is the engine that makes it go.

A third person is a woman living in a Lutheran nursing home in Nebraska. I'll call her Martha. I met her in a craft room where she was surrounded by quilting material. Though she had multiple mobility problems, her mind was intact, as were her eyes, fingers, and sense of humor. She made quilts that had a purpose: they were provided to newborns at the local hospital. She supplied hundreds of them. That's not all; she lived in a nursing home where most of the residents were mentally impaired. She gathered several of them together every day to help her with quilt making. She smiled, winked at me, and said, "Sometimes I have to redo some of their work at night, but we all help out." Martha exhibited the characteristic of *philanthropy*, continuously giving to others.

Dr. W. Candler Budd is my fourth exemplar. He was a United Methodist preacher, considered the founding board chair of Wesley Woods and a charismatic clergyman. Long after retirement, he and his wonderful wife, Dorothy, remained active in numerous causes. She taught piano until a few days before she died in her late nineties. Candler had a series of strokes that brought him to live at Wesley Woods nursing home. The last time I visited him, I opened with questions about his health. "How are you feeling? Are you able to eat more? Feed yourself better? Walk?" His response, in broken stroke-like articulation, "Fine. Fine. Now, tell me how your boys are doing." No organ recitals. Only interest in other people, their lives, families. No wonder people flocked around him and Dorothy. Candler exemplified a healthy attitude by maintaining his interest in other people and not himself.

A fifth exemplar. A friend's parents moved into a continuing care retirement community (now called life plan communities in many places). They lived happily there for several years until his father, then in his nineties, experienced multiple fender benders. No one was hurt, but it was an omen of possible tragedy to come. My friend and his mother appealed to Dad to give up the car keys, a hard decision, and often a power struggle. Because of the accidents, however, his father agreed to sell the car and not renew his driver's license. After all, the community had transportation to virtually every service and event he and his wife needed.

My friend visited a few months later. Driver's license was renewed, the car repaired. My friend was incredulous. "Dad, I thought you were giving up the car and license. It's dangerous for you to keep driving!" His mother could only roll her eyes and wring her hands quietly. Dad's response was, "I did some research on the Internet. I found out that most accidents occur while turning left. That's exactly how mine happened. My reflexes are not as good to turn left a lot. So I have programmed all the services your mother and I need by taking a right outside the retirement community. And by the time we get where we need to go and back to the community, we've made all right turns!"

Older people with a healthy attitude are *adaptable*.

Exemplar number six. One Saturday evening before bedtime, I received a call from the nurse in charge at Budd Terrace. The nurse asked if she could get reimbursement for the taxi fare for a resident who had just returned from dinner at a nice restaurant but didn't have money for the taxi. I said of course and told her how to submit the expense.

There was more to the story. Let's call the resident Hilda. As the story unfolded, this was not the first time the staff had been asked to pay Hilda's taxi upon her return from a nice dinner out. In fact, Hilda had developed a scheme whereby she called a taxi service she had not previously used to take her to a nice restaurant she had not previously patronized. She stiffed the taxi for the ride, the restaurant for the meal, and the return taxi back to Budd Terrace. Her activity finally caught up with her. Hilda was as poor as a church mouse. She lived at Budd Terrace on charitable assistance yet was determined to enjoy a piece of the good life. But now she was busted! You couldn't help but admire her creative scheming. Let's call her attitude characteristic *playful*.

George's mother, exemplar seven, was in her nineties, lived in the foothills of the Appalachians, and was a staunch, teetotaling Methodist, which is southern for "It's wrong to drink alcohol." Methodism was founded by an Anglican clergyman named John Wesley, who ministered to coal miners in England, where addiction to alcohol was rampant. For a century and a half, United Methodist doctrine opposed alcohol, but the Church has loosened a bit in the last fifty years or so.

George was a high-profile, successful public servant and business entrepreneur. He visited his mother frequently. On one such occasion, she commented that she had seen his picture in the society section of the Sunday Atlanta newspaper. She thought he looked handsome in his tuxedo and asked directly if he was consuming alcoholic beverages. He dodged by saying that the Bible says that Jesus drank wine, and, in fact, he reminded her that the Bible said Jesus reportedly turned water into wine at the wedding feast. George's mother quickly retorted, "Yes, but I would have thought a lot better of him if he hadn't." I characterize her attitude as *principled*.

Jean Probst, my eighth exemplar of attitude, was in her seventies when honored as Trustee of the Year at the annual LeadingAge Minnesota meeting a few years back. She had served as a board member of Episcopal Homes of Minnesota, which has served older people for 120 years. Episcopal Homes CEO Marvin Plakut reflected in his nomination of Jean that she had asked to meet with him privately after he had unveiled a draft of the organization's new strategic plan. Petite and soft-spoken, Jean opened the meeting with the comment, "I'm troubled by how small your thinking is, Marvin." Needless to say, the strategic plan was revised. Older people like Jean live with an attitude that continues to be *aspirational.*

Pilgrim Place in Southern California has been in existence for over a century. It was established to serve missionaries and other church workers who had no place to live following their missionary service. During my first visit there, I was invited to the residents' association meeting by one of their leaders, Elinor Powell, exemplar nine. I have attended many of these kinds of meetings. There are announcements about upcoming events, changes in rules, committee reports, and complaints. But this resident meeting was different in tone and focus. The Pilgrim Place brochure says that people move there "to continue their lifelong service and outreach to others." Noble words, but they came to life in Elinor's food committee report. I was looking for the common themes about food quality, variety, and temperature, but Elinor's "complaint" was that the Pilgrim Place community wasn't doing enough to contribute to a world hunger campaign that the association had decided to support. People with a healthy attitude in late life continue to be *engaged* in the world they live in.

Mother Mary, exemplar ten, heads up the Little Sisters of the Poor in Pittsburgh. Founded by Saint Jeanne Jugan nearly two centuries ago, the Little Sisters order has twenty-five hundred nuns in dozens of countries. They run their missions on philanthropy miracles. They ask and pray for money everywhere.

The Pittsburgh community is beautiful but financially challenged. Mother Mary said her lay trustee finance committee chairman lost sleep when they faced a payroll with insufficient funds on hand. When the chair expressed his distress, she responded, "When we need it, it comes in." Mother Mary is an exemplar of keeping difficulties in *perspective* and fearlessly so. Yes, a healthy older attitude offers all of us *perspective* and expects miracles. It happened that a Catholic layman down on his luck dropped by and asked for special prayers that a racehorse he owned would win an upcoming race. The horse was his last buffer from bankruptcy. He pledged that if Little Sisters prayed and the horse won, he would share the winnings. The horse won, and the Little Sisters' mission got money. Mother Mary received a knuckle-rapping letter from the Vatican. Her answer: "If you don't ask, you don't get."

And my final exemplar is Isaiah Moore of Minneapolis, who personifies the *contributor*. He received the LeadingAge Minnesota's Spirit of Aging Award in 2014. At the time, he was eighty-seven, lived in a senior community, and held down three jobs for his community. In his acceptance speech, he said, "Never feel like you're too old to do anything. That's the secret of successful aging." Legendary baseball great Satchel Paige, who pitched far beyond normal baseball years, once asked, "How old would you be if you didn't know how old you are?"

Those who age successfully are known for their...

Continued *passion*
Perseverance
Spirit of giving
Continued *interest in others*
Adaptability
Playfulness
Principled living
Aspirations
Engagement with others
Fearless perspective
Contribution

And yes, attitude is a choice. Virginia "decided every day" to tuck and keep walkin'.

Attitude is contagious. Older people who become victims of their diseases and conditions drive people away through stories of their festering sores or the quality and contents of their intake and output. They isolate themselves either in their homes or in institutions where like-attitude people congregate. Older people who are passionate, aspirational, engaged, and fun, and who express interest in others and continue to contribute are personality magnets for the young and old alike.

Intimacy

"...nobody ever touches me anymore..."

I'll never forget a lament of a Wesley Woods nursing home resident to her nurse: "Nobody ever touches me anymore. Oh, they change my diapers, clean and bathe me, but not real touching." She elaborated a bit that she missed hugs, strokes of the hand or hair.

Some older people miss sex. Taboo thinking makes it hard for some of us to imagine our parents, much less our grandparents, continuing intimate relations. These issues live in the land of denial, which creates outbreaks of intimacy that cannot be contained because the need for it is so strong.

By outbreaks, I mean episodes like that which occurred at Wesley Mountain Village in Blairsville, Georgia, in the beautiful foothills of the Appalachian Mountains. In the first year or so after opening, we had thirteen marriages, including two elopements. Some families were furious, calling to express outrage that we had "let our mother run off with some old man down the hall!" as one family accused me.

A dementia resident at Budd Terrace was an escape artist. He disappeared one afternoon. We notified family, police, and MARTA (Atlanta's public transit authority), but the man was a no-show all night. A frightful prospect for all concerned. The next morning, he reappeared, a bit disheveled in appearance but unharmed. A nurse asked him where he'd been, and he replied, "I spent the night with my girlfriend in [the nearby suburb of] Chamblee." The nurse asked her identity and address, and he replied, "Even if I could remember, I wouldn't tell you!" His lady friend had helped him escape, abetted by another resident who kept lookout. She dropped him off the next morning.

The first hint that sex was alive and well at Wesley Woods came in the first couple of months when I was the new twenty-six-year-old administrator. The Towers was among the first five or six Great Society senior housing programs known as HUD 202. A very successful concept: low-interest loan to nonprofit sponsors, three sizes of apartments, dining room, activity and health monitoring space, and beautiful grounds. All at reasonable cost, with subsidy funds for those with very low incomes. One of *the* best things the government has done for our aging population. But they have spent the last thirty years trying to kill the program for reasons still unfathomable.

The Towers also was a first in architecture: a round residential building. It won awards and was a flagship model for decades. It still serves and stays full over fifty years later, with loan paid in full. It was the vision of the late J. Scott Houston and the Wesley Woods board, including the aforementioned W. Candler Budd. Leaders from the Methodist Church and Emory saw the need to create senior housing and a nursing home in a campus arrangement that offered a continuum as people's needs changed. This concept was an innovative alternative to the prevailing "rest home" and/or "widows' and orphans' home" models that were scattered throughout the country at the time.

The Wesley Woods board started with the Towers and soon added a high-level nursing home called the Wesley Woods Health Center, followed soon thereafter by the building of Budd Terrace, which became one of the first programs now known as assisted living. The entire spectrum was available on one campus. The housing component was replicated in two other Atlanta neighborhoods, Athens, Augusta, and Blairsville, Georgia, in subsequent years. Today, these programs are commonly referred to as "senior housing with services communities." More of them are needed.

My first job at Wesley Woods was administrator of the Towers. I was in seminary right up the street at Emory and fresh from five years of working in a mental hospital as a psychiatric assistant on the evening and night shift. The mental hospital experience was a formative one in my career, as was the clinical pastoral education experience as an Emory Hospital chaplain intern. Both clarified my calling.

The mental hospital program was based on an emerging concept of institutional treatment called milieu therapy. A pivotal book called *Ego & Milieu* was a must read. It was based on principles of how to create healthy institutional cultures. An analogy to illustrate would be that the prevailing mental institution *and* nursing home approach was much like the classic movie *One Flew Over the Cuckoo's Nest*. The basic assumptions were that the inmates were crazy and had to be highly structured, medicated, and managed. Milieu therapy assumed people had a measure of ability and sanity and wanted to be healthier by exercising more control over their lives. To support those beliefs, the environment had to change from sterile institutional to something much more homelike.

So, fresh from my milieu therapy experience, I started a couple of support groups. One was the Newcomers, which I personally led. Among the first participants—all women at the time—was an eighty-nine-year-old woman I'll call Edna. One day I was late to the meeting. When I arrived, the dozen or so women were giggling, as if they had a secret. I commented, of course, and Edna said, "You have kept your harem waiting." They all laughed. I responded with an apology for my tardiness and chuckled about having a harem. Edna commented, as she clinched a lock of hair between thumb and forefinger, "Young man, this isn't mine [meaning her hair]. This isn't mine [pointing to her glass eye]. And these aren't mine [tapping on her front teeth]." Then Edna motioned her hand from neck to waist and declared, "But from here down, it's still all me!"

We all laughed. I got the point. A subtle reminder that needs last a lifetime. I responded, "Well, ladies, I will go home tonight and remind my wife not to take me for granted because *I* have a harem."

My late mother was one of the early volunteers at Wesley Woods and became more involved after I became associated with the organization in 1973. She especially did well with Alzheimer's residents at Budd Terrace, until she got burned out. She later read humor books to visually impaired folks. Favorites were books by southern humorists and columnists Lewis Grizzard, Ludlow Porch, and Celestine Sibley.

One day, a few months after my father died, Mother called me to come over to the house to discuss something important. The topic was her decision to move into Wesley Woods Towers. They had called with *just* the apartment she was looking for. I didn't know she had applied. She said it was none of my business, even though I was president of the entire organization by then. After moving in, she was elected as a floor representative and became head of the loyal opposition party to the administration. Some of the traditional rules were just too rigid, in her view, and she was committed to changing them.

One day I took her to lunch at one of her favorite greasy spoons. She had a loud, deep voice. She would remind you of Maude, yet with a Scarlett O'Hara southern belle twang. As we were ordering our meal, she declared, "Lawd, son." (By the way, anything that comes after "Lawd, son" in my family is like reading the King James red-letter edition of the Bible where *the* most important points come after "Verily, verily, I say unto you…" What follows is Gospel.) So, she began, "Lawd, son…I got elected floor leader. A bigger job than I thought. And…[she looked over her glasses, another sign of the importance of whatever message came next] you would not *believe* what goes on in that place after dark! You ought to see some of them slipping in and out of each other's apartments. Half dressed. And they're not as quick as they used to be!"

Mother's voice, already well audible in the restaurant, went up an octave or two, and she further asserted, "Now, son, I want you to know I am *not* personally sexually active *myself* any longer at seventy-nine, *but* some of these dear souls still are!" Forks dropped all around us. Chuckles could be heard from tables far away.

My response: "Mama, I didn't want to know all that! Geez…!" I squirmed like a worm in hot ashes.

"Well, you ought to know, son. You run the place."

Numerous examples of sex outbreaks (better than influenza or bedbugs, I suppose, as I look back): A man who hired hookers until he ran out of money and started bouncing checks. A woman who was a hooker at eighty and had a steady traffic of clients that came up the back stairwell left propped open at night. Only a new security alarm system exposed her business. She coyly said she would continue her profession. We advised her that if she had income she had not declared to HUD for her rent subsidy, she could go to jail. Whether or not she retired from her profession remains a mystery. Another man who visited a resident for amorous trysts mistakenly assumed the emergency chain in the bathroom was the fan. So, he and his lady friend were caught in the act, embarrassed by fire and rescue response that barged in.

Sexual intimacy takes on a more sober and reflective dimension when brain impairment is involved. A component of that reflection is the personal ethical dilemma that couples may feel when one is seriously impaired. Is the impaired party able to consent? Are they just being used?

My wife and I enjoyed a river cruise a few years ago. During a shore excursion, we wound up at a German pub lunch table with a couple in their mideighties. I assumed they were married. She was dressed to the nines and had a fixed smile and immovable facial features. He answered all the questions. They lived down the hall from each other in a senior community and took frequent trips together, he said. She seemed incapable of conversation, a combo platter of Botox and dementia, I surmised. But they were enjoying each other, getting out into the world.

On so-called dementia units or memory neighborhoods, sexual expression is common. Keeping unmarried people apart is difficult, as is the concealment of masturbation when the urge arises, which is often, given the loss of inhibition that accompanies dementia. A thoughtful institutional program at the Hebrew Home at Riverdale, a one-hundred-year-old organization, received a grant to do training videos for staff and families on how to handle sexual expression without ignoring, punishing, or making fun of participants. More recently, the Hebrew Home has established a sexual expression policy and program in their nursing home where consenting adults can meet and retire to one of their rooms for uninterrupted encounters. All key parties, including families and physicians, help make the decision.

I remember two residents on Budd Terrace's Alzheimer's floor who could not be kept apart. Both still had spouses. Family and staff tension was high. It seemed that the only solution was to ask one of them to move. But an enlightened family member suggested the opposite: let them move in together. Neither actually recognized their spouse any longer and yet enjoyed each other's company. Lots of emotional and ethical processing to be done. Yet both legal spouses believed their relationship as they had known it was over: "so long as love shall last." The solution worked well, and each of the parties affected could live with it.

Though hard to talk about, sex is important through the life span. Masters and Johnson concluded that it is possible at any age, assuming relatively good health and an interested and interesting partner. In fact, orgasms are correlated with lower blood pressure, less depression, better sleep, more effective pain management, and a more positive attitude.

But intimacy is broader than sex. It involves touching, hugging, hand-holding. It can include massages, mani-pedis, days at a spa given as a gift certificate. It can include fitness training for seniors. We all like a "Buffy" or "Biff" assisting us with firming up those abs. Perhaps the most popular intimate encounter takes place in the hair salon where intimate stories are told in the midst of feel-good scalp attention. Dancing, even wheelchair dancing, is a long-standing, satisfying, intimate experience that can include intergenerational encounters.

Intimacy also involves storytelling about memories of romance, or the birth of babies, or deathbed good-byes. Remember the movie *Titanic*, an intimate story of romance that kept all involved in rapt attention.

Intimacy is a key part of religious ritual in communal expression like Holy Communion or Passover Seder. And don't forget the importance of confession, potentially one of the most intimate conversations any of us ever have. The need for confession and forgiveness is lifelong, whether in the confession booth or from a barstool—to priest or bartender. We all question whether our life has been worth living. Those answers often emerge in confession, prayer, meditation, counseling, the most intimate of encounters with others.

Pets play a significant role in fulfilling intimacy needs, especially cats and dogs. One senior community that I visited in Oklahoma had an Alzheimer's golden retriever. It sought out residents who were acting out. The dog evoked a stroking impulse that golden retrievers love and calmed down the resident. A LeadingAge member in Rhode Island has a hospice cat that comforts people in their final hours of life.

The opposite of intimacy is isolation. It can be deadly. A woman was admitted to the Wesley Woods Health Center from a hospital. She had been found unconscious by neighbors who had not seen her in several days. The cause of her unconscious state was that she had stopped eating. One of our nurses asked her why she had done so. She replied, "I was so lonely, especially at dinner. So, I set up a table mirror for companionship while I ate. It didn't help. That's the last I remember until I woke up in the hospital."

The danger as we age, especially if we need long-term health-care, whether at home or in a licensed community, is that intimacy dries up. It is often replaced by either total isolation and/or clinical procedures, medicines that take the edge off our passions or, even worse, physical restraints. Never underestimate the drive for intimacy. It is a pervasive, lifelong quest that provides a flowing stream of daily fulfillment if we permit it to do so. And never ask a surviving spouse to make a deathbed promise that they will never be intimate with another partner. Such a promise can leave the survivor with anger over the shackle of celibacy allowed to be placed on them or guilt for breaking that promise. Anger and guilt over a number of years create ill health, laced with bitterness and regret that can affect generations.

Two important byproducts of intimate exchange are essential to successful aging: laughter and tears, both of which have psycho-logical, social, and physiological benefits. So let's explore whether to laugh or to cry.

Whether to Laugh or to Cry

"...more erotic than this..."

Early in my career, I was asked to be on a panel about humor and aging at my association's annual meeting. One panelist was a distinguished gerontologist named Dr. Ted Koff, known for his humor. The other was a psychotherapist from New York. I don't recall his name, so I'll call him Dr. Freud, whom he resembled.

Dr. Freud opened the panel with the story of an older patient who was suicidal. The man had lost his wife and was living with his son and daughter-in-law. Dr. Freud said the man's mood had brightened but cautioned the family that sometimes, suicidal people have brightened moods just before they kill themselves because they are relieved that they have made a decision. Suicide rates among older men are high. The most susceptible are men who have lost job and spouse.

The man's son and daughter-in-law felt comfortable leaving the old man for a long weekend because they thought he was "better." Then, late that weekend night, Dr. Freud's phone rang. It was his patient, laughing uproariously. Dr. Freud inquired what was going on. The old man said, "Doc, I decided to kill myself tonight. My family is out of town. They won't be back in time to save me. I filled the tub with hot water. I had a razor on the edge of it. I stepped into the tub and was about to sit down and slit my wrist when I had an urge to take a shit. So, I got out of the tub, sat on the commode, and began to do my business when it struck me: I've interrupted my own suicide to take a shit! Isn't that funny? I must want to live after all." More laughter. And live he did. Dr. Freud went on to extol the therapeutic virtue of humor and laughter as we age.

Let's distinguish the difference between making fun of old people, laughing with old people, and finding humorous twists in aging situations.

Making fun of older people, a class of people, is a form of "ism." Racism, sexism, ageism, classism. Jokes about Poles or Italians or southerners or people with mental or developmental disabilities or people who are overweight. Even people with Alzheimer's went through an era of jokes. I remember a journalist giving a speech to my Atlanta Rotary Club at Easter time. He introduced it with a joke that people with Alzheimer's could hide their own eggs. Yes, there was laughter, but I cringed as I looked around at faces of Rotarians whose spouses or parents with Alzheimer's my organization had helped. They weren't laughing.

Jokes about incontinence and adult diapers and impotence abounded in the genre of humor about growing old. Geezers or crocks or coots or hags have been common labels of degradation. We make fun of what we fear most, unfortunately.

Role models of a more authentic view of older people began to change with *The Golden Girls* and the Wendy's "Where the beef?" lady. These women were alive, vibrant, irreverent, funny. In recent years, Betty White has symbolized how older women can be really funny and hold their own in social situations. The late President

Reagan, our oldest president, chided his opponent Walter Mondale for his relative youth and inexperience. Perhaps we have turned the corner on ageism, but there are still far too many stereotypes that make fun of old age.

When I talk about finding the humor in the aging experience, I'm not referring to making fun of anybody. I am talking about laughing *with* older people. I heard a brain scientist on a talk radio show say that laughter is the shortest distance between two people.

The late Betty Barge, a Wesley Woods board member, told us of an older friend in the last stage of cancer. Part of their relationship involved the sharing of dirty jokes. Betty made a final good-bye deathbed visit. They prayed, shed tears. Betty was about to leave when her friend said, "Haven't you forgotten something?" Betty was at a loss for words and asked, "What?" The friend said, "You haven't told me a dirty joke." Betty, taken aback, retorted something like she was not thinking about dirty jokes at her friend's deathbed. Her friend said, "Until I die, I want you to tell me dirty jokes." Betty complied, resulting in a final good laugh to complement the final tears.

Creating occasions to laugh and cry together is essential to successful aging. We are all familiar with the importance of grief recovery groups, yet too little attention is paid to laughter group opportunities, even with people who are physically ill and/or cognitively impaired.

Back in 1991, the Atlanta Braves began their mythical quest from "worst to first" place in the National League. Someone gave our organization a block of tickets for a game. They were on the third base line and included part of two rows. Our staff decided to invite independent living residents, along with dementia residents. Of course, there were staff and volunteers in tow to assist everyone.

A group of young men sat to the left of our crowd. The beer vendor came down the aisle hocking cold Buds, whereupon one of the young men raised his hand and passed his money down the row of our people to the beer vendor, who poured the Budweiser in a tall souvenir cup and began to pass it back down the row to the young man who purchased it. The beer got as far as an Alzheimer's resident, who received it from the person on his right. He stared at it, then took a couple of sips. Since it had been passed to him, he passed it to his left, whereupon another Alzheimer's resident repeated the ritual, took a couple of sips, and passed it on.

Our staff was not quite sure how to intervene, but before they could, the young man looked down the row and declared, "That's OK; everybody have a sip and pass it on down!" Which they did. He received half a beer but gold stars for his good spirit. (He ordered his next beer from the other aisle.) Everyone involved got a chuckle out of it. They found the humor in it. Not making fun, just finding the humor.

The late Dr. L. Bevel Jones, "Bev," was a retired United Methodist bishop. He was one of the best pulpiteers I have ever heard. His secret sauce was his use of humor to make the deepest of points. Bev and I became close friends. Dementia ran in his family, and he was deathly afraid of it. He talked about it every time we called or saw each other. Bev and his wife, Tuck, became like family.

Bev and Tuck had a storybook teenage romance. He the ever-popular young Renaissance man destined for the ministry. She the blond homecoming queen. She died a few years back, and he became a gnarled shadow of his former self in a nursing home until his recent passing.

As they aged, Bev and Tuck went through a series of health problems. They would call when they weren't sure about who best to call on for help, especially when they faced the possibility of moving out of their home into a structured setting. Their health situation and relationship became complicated over several years. One would be back on his or her feet and the other would have a crisis. Back and forth. This dynamic put stress on their marriage and their family.

One time, when it was Tuck's turn to be sick, Bev called me to update. He always had a funny story and expected one of me. He always wanted to know the inside scoop from Washington, since I had become well-grounded in the politics of two White House administrations. He reported that Tuck had been in the hospital but was home. Then he said, "Larry, I was helping Tuck go to the toilet, and I kneeled down on the floor in front of her as she shuffled her way to sit on the commode. I looked up at her as I began to pull down her underpants, and I said, "Ya know, Tuck, I remember this experience being more erotic than this!" They found the humor in it.

A dear friend and colleague at LeadingAge, the late Susan Weiss, shared a memo from a member of her family back in rural Wisconsin. The family had done a great job over a period of years of caring for their parents at home. It was difficult for all concerned, but they had a loving and responsible family. Their father had recently been hospitalized amid steady decline. A sister back in Wisconsin was primary caregiver and had taken the father into her home. I received the following e-mail from Susan:

> I just got this from my sister at home. Some idea of how things are going with my dad home from the hospital… They're having fun now…!
>
> "To easily remove wax buildup on kitchen floors, empty one full catheter back onto floor, and wipe up with numerous bath towels. No need to let it sit for any length of time. Removal is instantaneous, especially effective if done during supper."

Finding the humor.

It is easier to find the humor in other people's situations than your own, but my wife, Kathleen, became a master of it with her parents. Both had multiyear health problems that Kathleen, her sister, Ros, and her brother, Larry, had to manage from a distance. The parents lived in Dallas, Larry in Austin, Ros in Boston, and Kathleen in Atlanta. The children did all they could to help their parents stay at home: live-in caregivers, home renovations, financial managers, planning of family events and activities that kept the children and grandchildren engaged, and rotation of visits. It was all very stressful at two hundred, seven hundred, and one thousand miles away.

Following one of her mother's surgeries, it was Kathleen's turn to be at the hospital. Anesthesia had a particularly peculiar effect on her mother. She could sound lucid while conveying delusional scenarios. On one visit to her in the hospital, she declared to Kathleen, "Did you hear that Spain has declared war on the United States?" Kathleen admitted she had not heard that news! Her mother declared, "Oh yes. And they have told us here at the hotel to stay in our rooms to be safe; however, I think we can beat Spain. We've done it before."

On another occasion, Dorothy told Kathleen that she had had a good day in therapy. She said her physical therapist was a black man, whom she liked. She told Kathleen that she confided in him about a family secret. First, she asked this black man if he was black. He confirmed that obvious status. Then she proceeded by sharing with him that her husband had been overseas during World War II and the Korean War. She told him she had reason to believe he had fathered a child by a black woman and asked the therapist's advice about how to approach the subject and perhaps track down her husband's wartime daughter. Kathleen expressed matter-of-fact surprise to her mother and offered to help find her half-sibling when her mother got out of the hospital.

Kathleen called Ros and Larry for her daily report on their mother's progress and matter-of-factly disclosed the good news and the bad news: the bad news was that their daddy may have fathered a child by a woman with whom he'd had a wartime fling. The good news was that they might have an additional sibling caregiver! All had a good laugh about it.

There were also humorous instances with Kathleen's father. Like the West Indian caregiver with a beautiful Caribbean accent who mistook Ros's direction that Mr. Wright liked the television show *West Wing* to mean that he liked "wrestling." The confusion became apparent on a visit where a wild and crazy wrestling show was on TV. Daddy had thought the caregiver wanted to watch wrestling, so he deferred to her choice.

On another call, Mr. Wright told Ros that he had decided *not* to marry one of his caregivers because he would feel unfaithful to his beloved wife, even though she was deceased. We still don't know how *that* confusing scenario penetrated his mind, but it was fodder for amusement in an otherwise difficult and wrenching situation.

But my favorite finding-the-humor story involves two (now deceased) colleagues and friends at Emory: Jim and Mort—Dr. Jim Fowler and Dr. Mort Silberman. Jim was a theologian and expert in the area of faith development and ethics. He established the Emory Ethics Center. A big man, quiet and reflective.

Mort was a world-class political operative representing Emory and a member of the Veterinary Hall of Fame. He was *the* most colorful character I have ever personally known, and an advocacy mentor. He cussed like a sailor. I made numerous trips to Washington with Mort. We never entered the office of a member of Congress or a US senator but that Mort wasn't immediately greeted and guided into the office for time with the principle elected official—whether from Georgia or not. Mort had advised presidents, kings, corporate CEOs, and Mafia dons about their exotic animals or cattle herds.

Mort had emphysema, from which he eventually died. Jim died from Alzheimer's disease.

My hallowed ground moment with the two of them came at an Emory VIP luncheon where the three of us sat together. I engineered the table seating. Mort needed Jim's support. You see, Jim's mother was an early-onset Alzheimer's victim and had lived at Budd Terrace for twenty years. He and his family had become seasoned veterans in dementia care.

Mort's mother had been recently diagnosed with dementia and moved to Budd Terrace. His mother was always difficult and demanding, now within a demented personality mind-set. She was driving Mort and his wife, Donna, crazy, and they were driving our staff crazy. Nothing was right. Mort's health was at risk. He had hypertension and a bad heart and was managing the aftermath of an experimental lung-reduction surgery that made his health precarious.

I gave Jim a heads-up about Mort's situation and asked Jim if he could establish rapport with him for mutual support. As we sat for lunch, I introduced them and casually told Mort that Jim's mother was at Budd Terrace and their mothers lived on the same floor. They shook hands, whereupon Mort immediately launched into his frustrations over his mother's care. He worked himself up to a red-faced lather.

Jim listened, then responded, "Mort, I've been where you are. It's a very frustrating disease. The staff is trying hard to please you and her, but it's impossible. So, I learned that taking a deep breath and finding the humor in the situation has been my salvation. I'll give you a recent example. We brought my mother to our house last Thanksgiving for dinner. She was a mild-mannered Quaker lady who now cusses like a sailor at times.

"She didn't seem to know any of us over dinner, but she was there. We all held hands around the dinner table and I was about to pray when my mother, her eyes closed, recited word for word an old Quaker blessing she remembered. We were all stunned of course, but pleased.

"It occurred to me that she still remembered her faith to some degree, so a few weeks later I took her to the Emory holiday concert at the Canon Chapel. They have a world-class organ and organist, and I thought the music and drama of it would be appealing to her. This particular concert featured Bach and involved recitation of the scriptures from Luke about the procession of the three Magi. The music played, then stopped. A faculty member in costume recited scripture, followed by more music. Then the second Magi walked down the aisle. The music stopped. He recited more scripture. Then more music.

"The third Magi processed. The music stopped and the Magi's recitation was a question rather than a declarative statement: 'Can this be the Christ child the world has awaited?' Whereupon my little Quaker mother asserted to those assembled, 'Well, of course it is! Any dumb son of a bitch knows that!'"

Mort's demeanor went from anger to laughter. In fact, he almost lost his breath. I never heard any more complaints from Mort about his mother's care. Jim had found the humor and began to help Mort find it as well.

All these situations could be cause for tears. Tragedy emanates from all of them. Yet, as one family member told me, "If I couldn't laugh about my situation, I'd cry all the time."

Growing old offers the opportunity for developing a self-deprecating sense of humor. A new nursing home resident at Wesley Woods was responding to questions by our nurse about his preferred daily routine. He replied with a twinkle in his eye, "I wake up every morning promptly at seven a.m. I like breakfast at eight a.m., and I have a bowel movement on schedule at six a.m." He grinned.

An older friend commented on his declining sex life, "I feel as good as I always did—just not as often."

Belly laughs and hard, sobbing cries come from the same place deep in the abdomen. When you have finished either, you will note a relaxed calm that radiates throughout the body. The physiological and psychological benefits are correlated with better health.

But laughing and crying are gifts to be nurtured. It is easy to stuff tears back inside for fear of never being able to stop crying. Many people have told me they won't let themselves grieve for fear of the inability to stop. But nature puts a governor on both gifts, and when we are spent, we stop for intervals of renewal, when tears are balanced by laughter. This balance is an important characteristic of successful aging. Perhaps the dying and death phase of life and aging is the most poignant experience and challenges our ability to laugh and cry.

But death truly loses its sting in the face of the discovery of humor in it. Read on!

Dying and Death

"...there comes a time..."

A colleague told me the story of the death of his one-hundred-plus-year-old grandmother. Grandma had a daily routine of breakfast, a walk around the block, tending to her garden, time with her two daughters, and a nap before lunch. One morning after breakfast, she declared to her daughter, "I'm going to lay down." Her daughter asked why. Was she not feeling well? Grandma responded, "I am dying." Daughter said, "I'll call an ambulance." Grandma declared, "Nonsense, call your sister to come over and hold my hand. I don't need an ambulance to help me die." Sister came over, and they all held hands. Grandma passed peacefully.

I made a speech at a large church's senior program. A hundred or so in attendance. The topic was whether to laugh or cry as we age. I asked the audience about laugh or cry stories. One man told of his mother's deathbed scene. Mother breathing her last few minutes. Family, kids and grands, standing around in reverence. Mother moved her head as if to ask for a sip of water. A daughter responded with a glass of water with a straw. Mother took a few sips, smiled, and looked each in the eye. Then came her last words: "A watched pot never boils." She grinned. She passed.

"O, death, where is thy sting?" No fear of death expressed. The last act no doubt passing the test of the play. Or, as I heard one grandmother put it, "I don't fear death so my grandchildren won't fear life."

Contrast those experiences with fights I've witnessed over jewelry on a dead mother's fingers, arguments over dosages of morphine in the final days or hours, conflicts over bequeathed possessions, unresolved sibling rivalry. Unspoken confessions. Forgiveness not offered.

I believe there are many patients in ICUs not because there is a chance that their condition can be improved, thus prolonging life, but because there are unresolved conflicts among families who are prolonging death. Rather than allowing a death with dignity and minimal suffering, there is death with unnecessary medical interventions and tensions, which extends personal angst far into the future.

I was fortunate to be at the bedside of both my mother and father when they died. The days' and weeks' run-ups to their deaths were very different. Mother's last days began in the oncologist's office. They ended with the aforementioned Dr. Eley at her deathbed. Dr. Lawson is a great physician and was Mother's oncologist. Mother had a rare form of "wild card" cancer, as Dr. Lawson described it. It is called Merkel cell carcinoma. It usually shows up on the skin and in the glands. Surgery forestalls it. Then months later it comes back and "runs" to other parts of the body unpredictably. Emory's Winship Cancer Center had seen very few cases of it. There were no effective treatments and no clinical trials. Mother and Dr. Lawson experimented but with no success. Kathleen and I went with Mother to Dr. Lawson's office to evaluate where she and the cancer stood after multiple surgeries. Mother (and Daddy) had durable powers of attorney for healthcare and advanced directives. Having those decisions in writing made my responsibility so much easier. I cannot emphasize enough the importance of these documents.

We sat in Dr. Lawson's office. Merkel cell had raised its ugly head for the fifth time. He and Mother talked about options. He offered very aggressive chemotherapy that had no evidence of promise except for difficult side effects. She asked if it could give her another several months, or even years. He said he doubted it. She said, "Dr. Lawson, I'm not afraid of death so much as I don't want to miss life: my grandsons getting married and having great-grandchildren. I don't want to miss anything." He understood. He'd obviously been at this hallowed-ground moment with many others. Then she said, "If you can't give me more quality years, then I'm willing to go into hospice if you can make me comfortable. So, you and Larry decide from this point forward...Now let's talk about something else." She died a few months later, family at her side, having said our good-byes.

And the last few months, talk about something else we did! She shared family secrets and lore. She talked frequently with grandsons John and David, entertained family and friends, and volunteered by reading humorous literature to the visually impaired at her home at Wesley Woods Towers, where she continued to be a nuisance to the administration.

Somewhere during this period, she had her head shaved at the Towers' beauty parlor. Then, at a residents' association business meeting, she doffed a French beret (she had several stylish ones, which we began to call her "cancer chapeaus"). Kathleen kept her in designer headwear, as Mother prided herself on her own sense of style. At the open-mic time of the meeting, she stood up and declared, "I want everyone to know I'm wearing these hats because I shaved my head because of cancer. So, I hope you men will stop hitting on me. I'm bald!"

This era of Mother's life was uncharted territory for our family. She did *not* want to talk about it. Though she signed the advanced directives paperwork and clarified authority for decisions, she was often secretive about the daily aches and pains cancer causes.

During this time, Mother did a lot of what the late Dr. Robert Butler, world-renowned geriatric psychiatrist, called "life review." Relaying, on a very measured basis, stories about family and friends. Some of her stories were gossip, like friends whose son and daughter-in-law's marriage was "never consummated, bless their hearts!" So, they got an annulment, he remarried, and he fathered children to whom we were distantly related. Mother quipped, "So, I guess he *finally* figured something out." Or another dear friend's son who was "a Jerome in the process of becoming a Melissa."

I reacted to such revelations with, "Mother, how in the hell do you know whether somebody's marriage has been consummated?" Her response: "Both their mothers talked with me about it. Lawd, how they grieved, bless their hearts."

During these last months, Mother would pass on pictures or pieces of jewelry that had sentimental value and say to whom they should be given. There were always notes attached giving details of why they were important.

She gave me two photos of the "old home place" in Greenville, Georgia. She asked if I could tell the difference between them. I couldn't. She instructed, "One picture has a coat on a hook right next to the front screen door. The other one doesn't. The coat is a signal to neighbors that the corn liquor is ready for pickup."

This is how I learned that Papa Roberts, her father and my grandfather, and other kinfolks made moonshine to supplement their sharecropper income. Further exploration led to the revelation that my family made corn liquor for President Roosevelt. You see, the "old home place" was just a few miles from Warm Springs, where the president retreated for therapy for polio. He would often ditch his security detail to drive to "the shop," Unca Aubrey's garage in Greenville. Roosevelt would have a "Co-Cola with the boys." He had an affinity for "the boys," not only because of the moonshine but also because Unca Aubrey and the local blacksmith rigged Roosevelt's cars so he could drive them with his hands.

One of the keepsakes passed on to me was a Ball jar that was once, and perhaps often, filled with Papa's corn liquor.

After Mother died, I queried cousin Bubba and my last living aunt, Ain Jenny, for more details. I remember telling Jenny that Mother revealed our family's role as Roosevelt's supplier of illegal whisky and asked if she knew more detail. She became very quiet, paused, then asked, "Have you ever heard of Booger Bottom?...It's not on the map. It's down off the Greenville-Gay highway not far from the Antioch Baptist Church, where we used to have the annual Cato reunion [Mama Roberts's side of the family]." She explained further. "You see, Mr. Roosevelt would come to the shop and some of 'em [southern for a well-known but unnamed group of people] would take him to Booger Bottom for his moonshine." I was ecstatic. "You mean it's true! Our family made corn liquor for the president of the United States?!" A pause, then Ain Jenny said quietly and humbly, "I didn't say I was proud of it, son."

I later found out that "some of 'em" was my uncle V.H. and one of our distant cousins who would hop in the president's convertible and lead an entourage of kin and Secret Service to Booger Bottom.

Mother also gave me a photo of Unca Clarence Roberts, "Papa's younger brother," she said. He was sitting in a chair, chains around his legs, big striped prison attire similar to that worn in the movie *O Brother, Where Art Thou?* And a hat cocked back on his head where you could see the tan line of his upper forehead.

Of course, I inquired about Unca Clarence's predicament. "Way-ull," she started, "he came home early one day from planting crops and found his wife in bed with the man down the road. So, he went out to the smokehouse, got his gun, and walked into the bedroom and killed 'im. Papa said he shoulda killed 'em both because she was sorry." (Sorry and/or trashy were the worst labels you could put on anybody. Sorry is not used in the apologetic sense, but in the sense that denotes the worst kind of human being.) Mother continued. "Bless her heart…" I asked whatever happened to Unca Clarence. Did he spend the rest of his life in jail? Did he hang? "No," she said somewhat indignantly. "He served six months or so, and they let him out." "Six months!" I exclaimed. With a defensive response, she fired back, "Lawd, son, his crops had to be harvested, and he was left with little chillen [southern for children] to raise 'cause his sorry wife ran off to Florida."

I learned a lot about Mother's side of the family in these final months. She had a need to pass on the heritage, and I wouldn't have missed the receiving of it for anything. She helped me understand why some family dynamics are as they are. V.H., her youngest brother, was an alcoholic, as was older sister Olivia. In fact, they may have been bipolar. V.H. joined the navy and was on the USS *Oklahoma* at Pearl Harbor. During the bombing chaos, V.H. ingested a whole bottle of aspirin on impulse. The aspirin precipitated lifelong ulcers, he said. He also had a drinking problem before he joined the navy. It only got worse after Pearl Harbor. Alcohol eventually killed him.

It is especially gratifying when families can videotape stories. My niece, Laura Shapiro, has a particular affinity for older people and is an expert filmmaker. She did a video of my mother for my sons and their children: the great-grandchildren she never got to meet. Laura knew how to make Mother's personality come alive! The video is called *Mamie, the Movie.*

The one positive gift that a terminal disease like cancer gives us is time to wrap things up if we take advantage of it. Hearing the stories and confessions, making amends, expressing appreciation, gaining perspective. Sorting out the important from the trivial. Yes, Mother and I had time. And the urgency cancer provided made us use it well.

So, don't waste the dying experience. It can truly be hallowed ground. And like the epilogue of a good mystery soap opera, it can really explain a lot.

Even if a disease isn't an urgent driver, making time and creating occasions to learn the family lore is a priceless process. Assume every time you visit or Skype or telephone that it is the last time you will interact with an older relative or friend. Then ask yourself: What do I want to know more about? What are the last words I want either of us to remember when we last talked? The conversation automatically changes!

Dementia complicates the long good-bye. Many terminal diseases ravage the body but not the mind and spirit. Alzheimer's is the fourth leading cause of death in America, and families often spend half a generation coping with a relative who has Alzheimer's. Collecting the family lore requires different techniques, often a guessing game of what a senior loved one remembers on any given day. Short trips to familiar places or important pictures or objects can be used as props or prompts. This can be hard and frustrating relationship work but can yield gold nuggets that pop up even as you pan through buckets of dirt without success.

The last time Michael Reagan saw his father, President Reagan, it was obvious to him his father was completely out of touch... *until* Michael got in his car to leave. He looked back, saw his father standing with outstretched arms. He'd remembered the need for his usual hug from his son as they said good-bye. Michael got out of his car and hugged his father. He had a priceless last memory, along with a reminder that dementia robs memory but leaves surprise remnants and flashes that are like those nuggets of gold.

The deathbed experience with my father was very different, in part because of his personality and in part because the disease that killed him was different. The last couple of days of Daddy's life found him in the ER of our local county hospital. I got a call that he was brought there by ambulance with acute cardiac distress. He would flatline, then recover. While Daddy had the "papers" delegating to me the decision to let him die without tubes, I did not have them with me. The hospital was suspicious of my motives and gave me a hard time about resuscitation. I threatened hospital officials with more shit (there's that word again) than they could stir if I rushed to the hospital and found him on a ventilator.

I found myself in the ER cubicle, watching Daddy arrest, come out of it, arrest again. Because hospital officials were breathing down my neck, I watched Daddy come out of an arrest phase, cradled his head, aroused him, and said, "Daddy, can you wake up to do some business?" He opened his eyes, responded, "Yeah, what is it?" I said, "These hospital people want to know if you want to be resuscitated if your heart stops and do you want to be on a ventilator?" He said, "Hell, no. You know I don't want that!" The hospital bureaucrats relaxed and left. I was free to honor Daddy's wishes.

Both John and David spent individual time with him and said their good-byes. They did a great job of it. Stories were retold. They both said they loved him and what a wonderful grandfather he was to them. He told them how proud he was of each and that he loved them. No regrets. Kathleen did the same. Daddy really admired Kathleen. She could get him to do things Mother and I couldn't, like quit smoking.

In fact, the deathbed makes some of the most hallowed of grounds, if you don't let medical machines, procedures, and bureaucratic professionals spoil the experience. This means that prior family communications and formal planning have to be put into effect. We did a good job of it.

It came to be my turn to stay with Da overnight and say good-bye. I tried to avoid it, but Kathleen wouldn't let me. It seemed much easier for me to let this man with whom I had experienced little deep emotional communication over my lifetime just drift into eternity overnight and await the call from the hospital that he had died. But Kathleen said no. She said it was my turn to stay the night with him—it would be his last. She said I *had* to say good-bye and I love you, whether or not he reciprocated.

So, there we were. Hospital room. Hospital twilight lighting. Heart monitor wires. Braves game—West Coast against the Padres—on TV. As I entered the room, Mamie and Da's minister, J.B. McNeil, was leaving. He said Daddy had asked him to pray for him and commented that he didn't think he'd last the night.

The minister left. Just Da and me. Awkward silence broken by the excitement of the Braves' broadcaster as the Braves scored. Da had another seizure, then awoke. Silence as he opened his eyes. All I could muster at that moment was, "What about them Braves?" He managed a "Yep" and a slight chuckle. I was looking for a door to deeper conversation, though it was totally unexplored territory. So, I commented on what a good man J.B. was. To my surprise, Da responded, "Yeah. He prayed for me."

Suddenly a door. I asked rhetorically, "He did?" Then I asked, "Do you ever pray for yourself?"

"Naw. Never have, I don't guess. I let other people pray. I'm not good at that." Another attack. Labored breathing.

Then I asked, "Would you like to pray for yourself?"

To my surprise, he said, "Yeah, I guess so…"

"What do you want to pray?" I asked.

"I don't know," he said.

"Are you scared of dying?" I asked.

"Yeah. Some, I guess," he said.

"Are you scared about where you are going?" I asked.

"Some, I guess," he said, then, "I don't know…I just don't want to leave here. But there comes a time for all of us."

So I suggested he repeat after me: "Dear Lord, I ask you to take care of me…I believe in you, but I don't understand much about faith…I believe Jesus came to help people like me…I ask your forgiveness for things I've done or not done [I asked him to list those silently in his mind and not necessarily out loud to me]…I am grateful for all you've blessed me with…I trust you'll take care of me…I'm in your hands. Amen." At points he would elaborate. I told him the Christian faith is just that simple and that he'd be OK.

"I've always felt I was in the hands of the Lord. And I've never had any doubts about anything about Jesus," he said. I had no idea about what he believed. I knew only that he went to church, perked the coffee, and counted the offering.

"But you have doubts about the other side of death?" I asked.

"I guess so," he said.

"Do you feel unworthy?" I asked.

"Yeah. I do," he said.

"Jesus died for the unworthy. If worthiness was a criterion to get to heaven, none of us could get in. You're going to be all right," I said.

"Yeah. OK…it's just the unknown. I guess I'm not so worried about the other side so much as I don't want to leave here. I've had a good life. Good friends. Good family…I'm proud of y'all. I've had a fine wife, smart. Can do anything. John and David have been a lot of fun. I've enjoyed the church and my buddies there." Compliments about Mother? Never before! I asked if he had any regrets. "No regrets!" he said. "And I haven't left any messes."

Keep in mind—he was having constant, interrupting seizures. Dim lights. Braves scored more runs. Then I asked him what kind of funeral he wanted. In keeping with his character, he said, "Keep it short and simple. People don't like those things." He wanted me to mention two individuals, the aforementioned Candler Budd, "a mighty good man," and the Reverend Jimmy Thompson, the pastor at the Belvedere Methodist Church who "saved several hundred of you young folks from smoking dope and sniffing glue."

I told him I'd miss him and that I had hoped he and Mamie could meet great-grandchildren, but I would tell Da-and-Mamie stories. He smiled and said, "Yeah, OK." I asked if we had more to discuss. "Naw." More seizures. He then said, "Hold me, Larry." I did.

Silence for several minutes. Then, "I'm OK now...the Braves won. Flip over to CNN and see how the Mets did."

"Let's try to sleep some," I said.

"Yeah, OK," he responded.

Early morning came. Mamie arrived. They talked privately. Then he said, "I'm ready to go," and he went.

A void was filled in me over those few hours. I learned so much about the enigmatic, self-contained character called Da, my father. He had faith I didn't know he had and doubts about himself that I suspect tortured him. He had more regard for Mother than I had ever dreamed. He was humble and "unworthy." I learned something about myself: my own avoidance of the experience, yet enough courage to jump in with awkward questions.

Now, let me tell you about Kay's deathbed experience with her mom. I believe it may be more common than is thought. It involves long-standing unresolved mother-daughter conflict, prolonged nursing home placement, and a coma. Not a good formula for resolving personal relationship issues.

Kay was a go-to staff member of my church, Decatur First United Methodist. She was what I call a Mother Earth archetype: full of compassion and energy. Kay became a member of the church support group called Dutiful Daughters, initially composed of women who cared for their elderly relatives at home. More about that later.

Kay had a lifelong, troubled relationship with her mother, who was distant and hostile. Her mom lived nearby, but the relationship was so estranged that Kay would have to leave groceries and meds on the stoop and drive away before Mom would come out to retrieve them. Kay never understood her mother's hardness.

As part of her role in the Dutiful Daughters, Kay wrote an essay about the story of her mother's dying. It is entitled "Waiting for Goodbye." Summarizing or excerpting from it would not do it justice, so here it is in Kay's words:

75

My mother died in a nursing home last spring. She was 88 years old and had been a resident there for over four years. For at least three of those years she was ready to die, and she and I waited longingly for that day, but in our own ways.

Once as I visited her with her nephew, who is a minister, she asked me to leave the room because she had some private business with him. Later he told me she had whispered to him to pray for her death.

Many older people sit quietly and wait for death. Others are more vocal. One dear neighbor of Mama's had a favorite request she made frequently to all who walked past her room, "Precious Jesus, take me home."

Sometimes it takes a long time to die—even if you weigh only 64 pounds and your tissue paper skin rips at the slightest touch.

In the last year of her life, I made a daily trip to visit Mama. I prayed each time that it would be her last day. How could she hold on so long? Her strong heartbeat defied her strong will to die. What was she waiting for? Finally, a helpful suggestion came from Larry Minnix, leader of a support group for people with aging parents.

"Sometimes," he said, "a person is just waiting for a goodbye from a loved one and then he or she will let go."

Mama had been unable to speak for over two years because of a stroke. She had not been out of her bed in almost a year. But I could never say, "Mama, I know you want to die, and I pray it will be soon for you." Until Dr. Minnix made his suggestion, I had not thought she might be waiting for my goodbye.

But I still wondered if she heard or understood when I talked to her. Her face never showed any emotion, no tears, no smiles. I would tell her of family events, what the great-grandchildren were up to, something about her friends. Each time as I left her I sang "Mighty Like a Rose" quietly in her ear.

So, I wrote out what I would say to her, not wanting to leave out anything important: my appreciation for her love and sacrifice through the years. That evening I laid my note on her pillow and read from it, wondering all the time if she heard.

A single tear rolled down her childlike face, and I knew Mama had heard my goodbye to her...and this was hers to me.

I wasn't there when she died a few weeks later. I was so thankful that I had said goodbye to her.

Not everyone is as fortunate as I was in the long good-bye with my mother or the deathbed reconciliation with my father. Nor as fortunate as Kay to have the insight and support to say good-bye so bravely in tough relationships.

My cousin Mike dropped dead of a heart attack just after he and his son had a huge argument where both said things they no doubt regretted. His son spent several years dealing with the unresolvable confrontation through addiction. Though he is currently in successful recovery, sudden death robs any of us of the opportunity for reparation and good-bye. Often the survivor of a raw and tragic last encounter finds themselves at a gravesite trying to make amends. This can be therapeutic, though it has an unfulfilled aftertaste.

Hohaus and Kay had the right idea: go to bed at night without being out of sorts with anyone you really love. Or write down good-byes and express them, even in the face of a coma. And make sure your last words to them are "I love you." So, if the phone rings in the middle of the night and a loved one is gone, you can at least remember the last encounter in a positive spirit—the last letter, the last I love you, the last hug.

Letters to and from family members can be a lasting way to reach healthy closure in the event of sudden death. Letters of love, advice, admiration—even apologies and regrets—are cherished possessions for generations in the keepsake nooks of family chests and dresser drawers. How we die and how family and friends face it with us is the ultimate test of the play. And the most hallowed of ground.

Dutiful Daughters

"...I don't know what you could have done..."

Thirty years ago, my church, Decatur First United Methodist, sponsored a "You and Your Aging Parent" education series. I was a presenter and talked about my observations about the biggest barriers preventing older people and their families from addressing aging issues satisfactorily.

After my presentation, five women approached me with one thing in common: they took care of their mothers at home. My speech resonated with them, so they asked if I would meet with them again to advise on coping with their situation.

Dutiful Daughters began. I met with them monthly for twenty years. Of course, participants changed as the years went by, and the group grew but had a steady participation of a dozen or so people each time it met. I handed leadership off to Chaplain Woody Spackman, director of pastoral services at Emory Healthcare. The group continues to this day as the Elderly Relative Support Group.

At our first meeting, the founders told their stories. Cathartic to them and enlightening to me. But they felt guilty about taking up my time and asked, "What's in this for you? Can we pay you?" I responded, "Ladies, here's the deal. I will tell you what I know and guide you to the best help I can refer you to. In exchange, you will teach me what it's like to care for older relatives at home. That will help me do better strategic planning for Wesley Woods." These women inspired the development of respite care, a geriatric evaluation service, an array of services to help people stay at home, and more community education.

In the early years, participants were all women. They began referring to themselves as Dutiful Daughters. Kay, whose story about her mother's saga was featured in the last chapter, joined one group and subsequently edited a pamphlet entitled *Dutiful Daughters*, which featured stories of several of these women in their own words, along with commentary by Kay of lessons learned.

Finally, the gender barrier fell. Ben, a single man, cared for his mother at home. And there were Peggy and Jim, the first couple. Peggy's mother lived in another state and had developed Alzheimer's. Her dad was committed to caring for her at home. Supporting Jim to support Peggy and her dad introduced the challenge of long-distance caregiving, increasingly common. Other couples joined.

Which brings me to Al and Marilyn.

Marilyn's mother needed help but had been verbally abusive to Marilyn all her life. Marilyn felt perpetually inadequate and guilty. Al gave her great support and reassurance, but she never quite believed that she wasn't a bad daughter. Then one Sunday morning, Marilyn and Al came to support group. She confessed she had taken their pistol from the drawer. She wasn't sure if she planned to shoot her mom, herself, or both, but she had unloaded it to put away the temptation. We did an intervention with Marilyn for psychiatric care that very Sunday afternoon.

Treatment helped Marilyn see that her mother was mentally

ill, demented, and mean. She began to believe Al when he told her she was really a good person. Marilyn had protected her own adult daughter from this trauma. Marilyn's therapist helped her understand that because her daughter's relationship with her mother was not emotionally loaded, her daughter could play a buffer role between them. Al and Marilyn began to take trips and have more fun. Their daughter assumed an important role with her grandmother. And Al and Marilyn became a source of support to other couples with similar experiences who joined the group.

Over time, members of the group became leaders of it. One was Linda Nalley, who was faced with multiple family challenges over the years. She was naturally therapeutic with others. Wisdom and an emotional intelligence are embedded in her genetic makeup. Bob and Linda Fleming joined. They were similarly constituted. Linda was called upon to use all her gifts when Bob developed Parkinson's and then ALS, from which he died. Just knowing these people over the years has provided me with continuous hallowed-ground moments.

Here are two of their own stories. They reflect the realities of what makes for successful aging. Some of their lessons for us are obvious; others are between the lines.

DUTIFUL DAUGHTERS, "An Entirely Different Person,"
by A. H. H.

My mother moved from out of state into our home about seven years before she died. Prior to that time, she had visited us each year from Thanksgiving to February. My mother and I were very close; I am an only child and Mother was a very domineering and fiercely independent person.

I felt like a guest in my own home when Mother lived with us. I didn't take the responsibility I should have. When I had a day off from work, I didn't stay home.

I began to realize that Mother was not keeping up with her finances and bank account. She would take the mail from the box and misplace it. She began to think we were stealing her money because her Social Security check went directly to the bank. One of the hardest things to do, I'm sure, is to give up the privacy and control of your own checkbook. That step came with Mother.

We fixed Mother's bathroom for her comfort and safety by adding grab bars, a bench in the tub, and a spray shower she could hold in her hand. Don't you know, she didn't like any of it!

The doctor recommended that Mother not take hot baths because of poor circulation in her legs. She interpreted that as "Don't take a bath." This became a problem that continued for the rest of her life. She never liked me to help her with her bath, nails, hair, or anything. She was indignant if I did anything about her personal care.

She was rude and insulting to her doctor. She was so ugly during one visit I almost left her there by herself. I was so angry and embarrassed about her behavior, yet I was so conscious of my upbringing. You were not disrespectful to your parents. This was your mother. You just took it.

The worst thing that could happen to anyone, according to Mother, was to have to live in a nursing home. That idea was just ground into me. It looked like your children didn't love you and were neglecting you. I always tried to reassure her. I had the feeling almost that I owed Mother a place in my home, the "dutiful daughter" coming out.

The older I get, the more sympathetic I feel toward my mother. When you move in with someone where living patterns are long established, everyone has to give a little; no, not a little, a lot. And older persons are so much less open to change. There's no way they can do it.

I never knew whether Mother was going to be gracious to our friends who dropped by. When an elderly parent is in the home, you need to keep your own activities in focus. Remember where your first responsibilities are and carry them out. Lots of times I did not do this. I just chickened out on the whole thing.

Once I took Mother back to her hometown to tend to some business. I was in a hurry to get on back home. "Aren't we going to ride around?" she asked. I thought, "Lord, I am so insensitive." So, we did ride around and see the old hometown. It's a fond memory now.

Mother needed to be busy and feel that she made a contribution to the household. It might be stringing beans or watching the crockpot. A scene that I remember vividly is Mother sitting in her favorite chair in the breakfast room, sweeping the floor.

Gradually Mother became very weak. The doctor said there wasn't anything we could do if she decided not to eat. He explained that a lot of old people decide they don't want to cope anymore, and they deliberately stop eating.

It was a terrifically hard thing for me to accept. I tried to make her eat. I tried everything. I would beg her; I would plead. I tried to shame her into it. She'd just look at me. I would feel so stupid, so angry with her.

One morning after several weeks, Mother fell in the bathroom and was too weak to get up. I was so frightened. I called my daughter, who is a minister. "Get the name of a good counselor, preferably a woman, right away and make an appointment," she said. And I did. I continued in therapy from October to February. Mother died in November.

I wouldn't take anything for that counseling. I needed help with what I was going through and what Mother was going through.

The doctor put Mother in the hospital for three days to force-feed her. She stayed for two weeks. When she was admitted, the nurse discovered that she had severely ulcerated, even gangrenous, ankles. Mother had tried to treat them herself and had been able to hide her condition by wearing slacks.

It came time for Mother to leave the hospital and I was faced with what to do. I had always thought that I would know a long time in advance if the nursing home stage was coming. I should have been visiting nursing homes, determining what kinds of cases they would take, fees, Medicare, etc., all of that. Instead, I had to do it in a hurry.

Thank goodness, I had visited Wesley Woods, and I had a much better feeling about nursing homes. When I called, they had space for her. But how was I going to tell Mother she was going to a nursing home? Dr. Minnix had suggested, "Just tell her you are going to try this for a week until her leg gets better." I don't think Mother ever realized that Wesley Woods wasn't just another hospital.

Mother had very good care there. When I visited, we'd make conversation. She was not eating. Many times, her meal would be sitting there untouched, and I would urge her to eat. "You eat it," she'd say.

I regret that I didn't go more often to visit Mother. I don't care what people say. Your hindsight still makes you say, "I wish I had done so-and-so. I wish I had. I wish I had been more patient."

I am worried that I will act the same way that Mother did when I reach that stage in life. My daughter tells me that I won't. "You are an entirely different person from your mother. You're not that way." Her words are very reassuring. Isn't that a valuable thing to know?! We are not the same people as our parents.

Mother had a lot of anger and bitterness bottled up inside her, and the cap just blew off in her last years. I was sad when she died, but I never cried. I was very conscious that, deliberately, she had starved to death. She called the shots about herself up until the moment she died.

Before she died, Mother did away with most of her personal belongings. After her death, I went looking for pictures, letters, etc., and they weren't there. The drawers were bare.

I'll never understand why. It was either her way of preparing for the end, or sometimes, I think she did it for spite. A few weeks before she died, Mother offered a tintype of her grandfather in his Confederate uniform to her nephew. He refused it. Later when I asked about it, she said she didn't know where it was. I knew that she put big bags of trash out for the weekly collection, but I never thought much about it. I knew that she subscribed to several newspapers and magazines and thought that was what was going out. Later, I realized that this was the way she had disposed of her personal things.

Mother was fortunate in that she did not have to stay in a nursing home for a long time. That was a blessing. I know too that I could not have made it without my husband's understanding and support. I love him so much for being thoughtful and willing to be a part of the situation. I feel sorry for anyone who does not have the full support and cooperation of her spouse in a similar situation.

I still have strong feelings of guilt about my mother. My husband says, "I don't know what you could have done that you didn't do." I know he's right, and I must keep telling myself that.

DUTIFUL DAUGHTERS: "Loved Me the Most," by F. T. F.

At age 87 my mother came to make her home with my husband and me. We had felt that keeping her in her own home as long as possible was best, and we did that with help for a number of years. As her health failed and symptoms of Alzheimer's disease increased, we chose to bring her into our home to live.

She was gentle, quiet, lovable, and as easy to care for as a person in her condition could be. However, we were not prepared for the changes in our lives that having her with us made.

My husband and I had just retired from our jobs and we had looked forward to having time to travel and pursue other interests. Of course, this was impossible now, because Mother could not be left alone. Consequently, we both became frustrated, and I began to feel conflicting emotions. I wanted to take care of my mother, and at the same time I felt resentment for having the responsibility.

My sister and two brothers helped with her care for a time, but as her condition worsened, I was not given the help or support I needed. This was very discouraging to me.

In retrospect, I realize this conflict with my family was as much my fault as theirs. I had chosen to care for Mother; thus, they saw it as my responsibility. I failed to expect or require enough help from them. If in the beginning the decision for Mother's care had been ours, rather than mine, and a plan made with all of us contributing and sharing, I think we could have avoided much misunderstanding and heartache later.

I cared for Mother because I really wanted to, even though I was drained physically and emotionally with her constant needs night and day. I felt tenderness and love for her and received a great deal of satisfaction in caring for her. I kept her clean, dressed her in pretty clothes, put a ribbon in her hair, and made her room attractive with pretty sheets. I used lots of color, plants and flowers, and potpourri for a nice fragrance.

It was particularly frustrating not to be able to communicate with Mother. There was so much she could not understand. But even in her confusion she never lost her gentle and cooperative spirit. She lived in a time long past, and I discovered if I took her seriously and entered her world too, I could often relieve her anxiety and give her comfort.

If Mother were worried about her mother (long deceased), we would talk about what we could do for her. If she concerned herself with some job in the past she thought she hadn't done, we would plan (pretend) to do it together, etc.

It was a challenge to cook and provide nourishing meals for her. I felt tremendous satisfaction in discovering new ways to prepare her food. One was a delicious fruit shake I would make for her by mixing several different fresh fruits and pureeing them in the blender.

Mother had difficulty chewing a tossed salad, and I learned to put all of the ingredients in the blender and serve it as a cold soup. There was no way she could get this kind of attention in a nursing home, and I wanted to keep her as long as possible. But I needed help!

One great help in learning to cope was the understanding our support group at church provided. We became a group of friends, all with aging parents, who almost felt like a family. We listened, we shared experiences, we cried and we laughed together, we supported each other and gave comfort and suggestions. Most of all, the understanding of our common problem helped us through these tedious and trying times.

More help came from Wesley Woods Health Care facility. When I learned they would take Mother for respite care, I felt a great load roll off my shoulders. I knew I had a place I could take her for a short stay. I could get a much-needed rest and have time to do some traveling. I found tremendous help also in having sitters come in for several hours a week.

The most special and appreciated help was from my husband. His love and support were never-ending. He didn't complain, but listened and understood when I complained. He let me cry when I needed to cry. He calmed me when I was overwrought. He learned to do almost everything for Mother that I could do, and she responded to him very well.

Our children were a source of needed support. They gave their "Granny" extra love and attention and showed in numerous ways how much they cared. They missed having us free to take part in their family activities, but they were behind us one hundred percent in what we were doing for Mother.

As her condition worsened her last year, we had to have nursing care part-time in our home. Then, the last six months of Mother's life, a move to a nursing home was a necessary decision, though very traumatic. In some ways, the experience I'd had with respite care at Wesley Woods took some of the fear away and helped me to make the change. At this point, Mother was aware of very little. I continued to look after her carefully in the nursing home, but they were able to give her nursing care that I could not provide at home.

Mother died peacefully at age 93. I had lost the one

person on this earth who loved me the most, but I was ready for her to go. I had given her more than five years of my life, but how much more she had given me!!

Though this was one of the most difficult periods of my life, it was a time of growth, of practicing patience, giving love and understanding, and receiving love. My faith was deepened, learning to depend more on God, and I was given an insight into family relationships I would never have had otherwise.

I have felt very little guilt, though I remember the times of despair, the times I was short-tempered and impatient. I see the mistakes I made and the ways I could have done better. However, I know I gave Mother much loving care and I focus on this, rather than dwell on what might have been.

I was blessed in so many ways and I am thankful to God for this time he gave me with my mother.

So, what about those "barriers" that the Dutiful Daughters found so resonant? Let's explore those in the next chapter.

Barriers

"... I just didn't want to bother you ..."

Why are aging-related family matters so difficult to resolve successfully? Let me tell you about nine major barriers with a story to illustrate each.

BARRIER #1—STUBBORN PRIDE: "Grandpa's Pistol"

Jane called, worried about Mother, Grandmother, and Aunt. Mother and Aunt had been in the hospital recently, each with stress-related problems. Jane said that Grandma was still living at home with Grandpa, who was demented and blind. Grandma was Grandpa's primary caregiver.

Grandpa became delusional that his wife was having an affair. One night, he sat by her bedside with a loaded pistol, threatening to kill her. He'd had a previous episode of wandering in the yard with a gun but was subdued without harm by the police. Grandma refused to admit him to a care community and refused to let others, family or friends, help her. It was *her* duty: "for better, for worse; in sickness and in health."

Jane's hope was that I could convince Grandma to institutionalize Grandpa before somebody got hurt. Both daughters, Grandma, and Jane met with me. The daughters spilled their souls with their frustrations about Mom's unwillingness to get help. Grandma sat stoically and listened. When the daughters finished their spewing, I asked Grandma if she knew they had these feelings, and did she realize that her stubbornness about Grandpa was affecting her daughters' health. She admitted she had never thought about that, though she knew they had been ill. I told her that, from my experience, her husband needed to be in a secure environment and reminded her that his brain disease could get her killed.

But she didn't think so. After all, the night he held his vigil with the pistol, she simply waited for him to fall asleep and gently took it from his lap, along with the other guns in the house, and hid them. He was *her* responsibility, and *she* was unafraid. "I just can't put him in a nursing home right now."

I asked her that if the pistol threat or her daughters' health wouldn't prompt her, by what criteria *could* she consider putting him in a "home?" She replied, "I've thought a lot about that, and my conclusion is that I can do it when he no longer knows my name." News to the daughters and granddaughter. They all cared but were never on the same wavelength about Grandma's criteria, and *why* she could not let go of Grandpa—the why being the fulfillment of her duty as a wife, however noble or dangerous. Some people have so much pride that they feel they must confront issues totally on their own terms without regard to the effects of *stubbornness* on others. But straightforward communication can *at least* achieve understanding and sometimes can help folks agree on a course of action.

Some people don't get help because they are too *stubborn!*

BARRIER #2—OVERWHELMING SITUATIONS: "Seventeen Shithouses"

Mr. Thayer brought his mother to Wesley Woods for therapy after a hip replacement. He liked the care. She had other complications that necessitated her being in a nursing home long-term. He wanted to keep her with Wesley Woods because he liked the care she received, but finances were an issue when Medicare coverage ran out.

Wesley Woods had charitable resources to help people like Mrs. Thayer, so I gave him an application, which required him to detail his mother's income and assets. He refused to complete it but nevertheless demanded that we keep her on charity. We denied the request, so he moved her.

End of story? No. Hardly. Months later, I received a call from Dr. Hand, a pastoral counselor and professor whom I respected. He was faculty at the Candler School of Theology, where I received my graduate degree. He asked if I remembered Mr. Thayer. I said yes. He said that he was treating Mr. Thayer in an alcohol rehab program. He elaborated that Mr. Thayer's mother had died in another nursing home and that Mr. Thayer blamed me for her demise. Dr. Hand understood what I had done and why. He went on to say that Mr. Thayer had lost his wife and son to cancer within the last few years. These tragedies precipitated the loss of a successful business. Then he lost his mother, who was dear to him. Dr. Hand said that Mr. Thayer was working through his rage about his plight and that simply expressing it to God was not enough. Dr. Hand said that I was the only living human being involved that Mr. Thayer could express his anger to and asked if I could hear Mr. Thayer out. It could be cathartic for him. I agreed to do it if it might help him recover.

Mr. Thayer came to my office. He used a cane. His demeanor

was flat, like the facial expressions of Jack Benny. He began calmly telling me of his saga and commented matter-of-factly, "I haven't thought of murdering you or anything like *that!* Even though you really murdered my mother." Hmmm…

As he unrolled his story, about which I had no idea, his voice gradually rose, and the intensity of his expression grew. The climax of the encounter came as he sat up in his chair, his back growing stiff, his hands gripping the chair arms to white-knuckle levels. *"So, you call yourself a clergy, but if God granted me the authority to make the decision about your ultimate eternal destination, I would bury you for an eternity under seventeen shithouses!"*

An emotional boil lanced. A resentment load of seventeen shithouses is a lot of anger. His demeanor changed. He sank back in the chair, folded his hands in his lap, and calmly asked, "Now, what do you have to say for yourself?"

I must confess my two initial thoughts were not particularly noble or therapeutic. One was that I was glad no gun had been pulled, and the other was, "Why seventeen? If I'm buried for eternity under shithouses, a whole different concept of hell, I admit, wouldn't twelve or even five do the job?"

But I verbally responded, "I am so sorry, Mr. Thayer. Your losses are unimaginable. If I had known then what I know now, I would have worked with you very differently. I am sorry."

"Very well, then," he said. He walked to his car—I saw him from my window—but then he returned to my office. I was wary. But he simply asked, "Say, I am in need of a good doctor, a geriatrician at my age. Can you recommend one?" Which I did and called the doctor's office with a request to fit Mr. Thayer into his patient load.

Some problems, like those faced by Mr. Thayer, can seem so overwhelming that people contemplate the unthinkable. However, there is *always* help available, even when overwhelmed. The Dutiful Daughters didn't face a problem that others had not faced or managed. More importantly, suicide or homicide are permanent solutions to temporary problems.

Some people don't get the help they need because they are *overwhelmed*!

BARRIER #3—THE HEALTH SYSTEM ISN'T HELPFUL ENOUGH: "Uncle Gene"

I got a call from Sydney, daughter of one of the founders of the Dutiful Daughters. As time passed, Sydney's grandmother died, and Sydney's mother became limited in what she could do for friends and family. Sydney and her husband, Bill, gradually inherited the caregiver responsibilities for family and friends, ultimately including both sets of parents, the late grandmother, a sister with cancer—which led to responsibility for nieces and nephews—and her children, along with Sydney's uncle Gene.

Uncle Gene had broken a hip, went to postacute rehab, and was discharged to home, where he lived alone. Sydney's mother tried to manage the situation but was unable to do so. Sydney naturally picked up the burden. Uncle Gene was difficult, irascible, stubborn, and alone. He needed to be in a sheltered environment but insisted that he go home. Sydney's mom had arranged sitters, but none lasted more than a day or two because of Uncle Gene's behavior.

Sydney thought she had found the right person, someone who seemed to have a good way with Uncle Gene, for a couple of days. Sydney went to Uncle Gene's home to check on the situation. She encountered the new sitter walking out, declaring that she couldn't take it anymore. She then proceeded back inside with Sydney, where Uncle Gene was lounging in the den in bra, panties, negligee, and slippers.

Sydney was stunned. She called her mother, who confessed that Uncle Gene had this "problem" and had suffered from mood swings for years. A skeleton in the family closet. Of course, Sydney, now feeling a moral responsibility for him, asked Mom, "Why didn't you tell me!" She responded, "Well, I didn't want to bother you with it. You have your own life to live." Sydney was blindsided, incensed, and frozen as to what to do. I told her there was help. Initially I said, "Here's the good news. First, his condition isn't contagious. Second, he won't go around the neighborhood trying to convert people to it. And third, his 'problems' open the family up to lots more Christmas present options for Uncle Gene."

I also told her that because of his mood swings, Uncle Gene sounded like a man with unmanaged bipolar depression. So, we secured him an appointment with a geriatric psychiatrist and admitted him to an intermediate care nursing home, in a private room, with staff trained on how to handle his behavior. Sydney was back in charge. Uncle Gene was stabilized and able to enjoy his lingerie.

Healthcare delivery is often not trained or equipped to manage subtleties like specialized care and services. So, families follow a traditional path of a discharge to home without the physician and hospital personnel understanding complexities. It is imperative that families themselves know the whole story and communicate to the professionals in charge. And the health delivery system needs to be more individually tailored to the needs of seniors.

Some people don't get the right help because of *health system design flaws*.

BARRIER #4—COMMUNICATION: "I didn't want to bother you…"

My late mother developed cancer in the last four years of her life. A rare cancer, it led to multiple surgeries and experimental drugs. Kathleen and I were in Washington, where we had relocated for my job, while Kathleen commuted back and forth so my mother and her father would perceive that Atlanta was still "home." We kept our Atlanta home until after both died.

I had taken a rare day off for us to see Washington sights. We had ordered lunch in a historic tavern in Georgetown when my phone rang. A voice I recognized as belonging to Doris, Mother's closest friend, whispered anonymously, "Your aunt called me. Your mother has been admitted to the emergency room. She'd kill me if she knew I bothered you with this." And hung up.

My day off to see some sights suddenly became ten hours of searching for Mother. No record in any local emergency room. Neither her internist nor oncologist had seen her or admitted her to any of Emory's hospitals. My aunt did not know which emergency room. And the staff at Wesley Woods Towers, where she lived, had not known of any transfer to a hospital. However, one staff member thought they had seen her at dinner and that she was in her apartment, which is where I finally contacted her.

The accounting for her whereabouts is unclear to this day. Best I could tell, she had some kind of episode. She called my Ain Jenny with some alarm. Jenny called Doris, who stewed on it a while and then thought I should know. In the meantime, Mother went to the outpatient clinic on the Wesley Woods campus, where she did not formally register as a patient visit because a nurse who knew her well gave her assistance and sent her back to her apartment, all under the formal radar of care delivery.

When I finally caught up with Mother, I scolded her for not calling when she had the episode. I had contacted three hospital ERs, and she immediately declared her intent to "kill Jenny and Doris for bothering" me with this. Not "bothering" me created a ten-hour bother from six hundred miles away that ruined my day off and created unnecessary stress for my wife, me, my aunt, and my mother's best friend.

"I didn't want to bother you" is a classic, often-used excuse for not keeping loved ones in the loop. Our personal health is a private matter, but families who care about each other need to know what's happening, especially when a known health problem can create crises that necessitate ER visits.

Some people don't get help because of poor *communication.*

BARRIER #5—DISCOMFORT WITH FEELINGS: "I think my mother is dying."

John is a brilliant attorney. He sought my advice about his mother. The opening volley: "I think my mother is dying of cancer, but I'm not sure. How do I talk with her about that?"

"Why don't you just ask her?" I queried.

"I'm an only child," he answered. "I grew up not talking about such matters. Our family dinner conversations were about intellectual pursuits. But never about things like this. When I finished college, I took a year abroad. When I returned home, I found out my father was near death with cancer. My parents hadn't told me about it. He died, and I didn't have the opportunity to tell him good-bye. I asked my mother why they had not told me about his condition. She said [you guessed it] that they didn't want to bother me with it and ruin my trip. So, if my mother is dying, I am determined to talk with her about important things. I just don't know how. Can you help me?"

I suggested he start simple. "Mother, I love you, so I need to know. Do you have cancer? Are you getting better, or are you dying from it? Have you thought about what kind of help you may want from me and my wife?"

Then, he should end the conversation with just what he told me: "I am determined to have a more meaningful relationship with you either way because I lost the opportunity with Dad. I love you very much, and I know that you and Dad have always loved me."

We actually practiced these questions and lines. He felt awkward, wasn't sure about this new language to be used in such intimate ways. I told him these kinds of communication are awkward at first, like talking with your kids about the birds and the bees, but it gets easier and more rewarding. He followed the advice. Yes, she had cancer, prognosis not good, but she died with a deeper relationship with her son.

Communicating on an emotional level is difficult at first with some people. It takes getting used to. "I love you." "I'm afraid." "I'm angry." "I'm confused." "I care." Hard communication barriers, but once crossed, it gets easier and much more personally satisfying, especially when the end of life is in sight. And assume it always is!

BARRIER #6—NOT KNOWING THE DIFFERENCE BETWEEN RESPONSIBLE *FOR* AND RESPONSIBLE *TO* SOMEONE: "Spots on His Pants"

Emily approached me after a "You and Your Aging Parent" session at a church. Her mother had died within the last few months, and she had concerns about the changes she had seen in her father and what she should do about the situation. Did he need a nursing home? Should she move back home to care for him? Did he have some kind of illness? Should she make a doctor's appointment?

Usually a dapper, neat dresser, Emily's father was now unkempt. He had spots on the front of his pants and he smelled like stale urine. He had stopped socializing, even with his men friends. He was occasionally confused. But there seemed to be no clear and present danger. And his condition seemed to correspond to the death of his wife. He was grieving.

I suggested to Emily that she treat her father like the man that he was and share her observations. Tell him she did not want to run his life, but she was concerned that he might be depressed from grief and/or that he had some kind of subtle health problem that caused the soiled pants and odor. Yes, it's hard for family to talk about body odor at *any* age, but after all, he was a man. Then offer to help set up a doctor's appointment for *her* peace of mind, if not his.

She had "the talk." He admitted he missed his wife terribly. He was aware he had withdrawn from friends but wasn't aware of the spots and odor. The doctor confirmed depression, but also uncovered a urinary tract infection. When treated, it cleared up quickly. The infection caused the hygiene symptoms. He was back on track.

To suggest a nursing home, or even a move back home, put this daughter into caring *for* her father prematurely. So, how should she be responsible *to* him? I asked if they had a history of good, straightforward communications throughout their lives. She said they had. I asked her if her father and mother had talked openly about uncomfortable things like sex or family finances. Yes, they had. To take charge prematurely is paternalism. To ignore can be irresponsible. To become the adult child creates a new relationship dimension between parent and child.

Jane was responsible *to* her mother, aunt, and grandmother. Sydney had to become responsible *for* Uncle Gene. John was responsible *to* his mom. Emily learned how to be responsible *to* her dad.

Confusing these types of responsibilities can lead to comical disaster, as with this story of a man and his pickup truck. A family decided it was time to move Dad to Budd Terrace because he had become confused. They sold his beloved pickup truck in the process. He kept escaping from Budd Terrace, only to be returned by the police or MARTA. One day, he drove himself back in a brand-new red pickup truck. He wasn't so confused that he didn't figure out how to buy a new one! Big life decisions made *for* him instead of *with* him. As another older man facing similar circumstances said to me, "When you mess with a man's car keys, checkbook, or a place he calls home, you're messing with his basic independence."

Some people don't get help because the feelings evoked around aging are a *new language* for many.

BARRIER #7—SIBLING RIVALRY: "The Little Prince"

Mary sat in our living room recently. She bared her soul on the recent death of her mother and the illness that led up to it. Her mom lived and died in another city, near her two brothers, one older, the other younger. The older brother is a lawyer and had the legal authorities needed to control Mom's business affairs and healthcare decisions. He resisted Mary's involvement in Mom's care, even though Mary was also an attorney and had taken her mother to a geriatrician for a comprehensive evaluation, which confirmed that Mom was demented. The conflict between Mary and her brother was initially over Mom's ability to drive.

The physician confirmed impairment, and documentation of this was submitted to the state where Mom lived to prevent her from renewing her license. But the brother had the decision reversed. When Mary informed her brother about the dementia diagnosis, he wrote her an email and said, "F--- off! Never talk with me again about Mom!" Her younger brother was passive about the situation. Mary's only support was her husband.

I call this the "Little Prince Syndrome," and I described to Mary how it works. She declared, "Yes! You must tell this story!"

There is a Little Princess version called "Diva Daughter" that plays out in the obverse. The Little Prince is a controller. The Diva Daughter is a know-it-all. Both make decisions or second-guess decisions of others. But the ultimate outcome of either behavior has chilling effects on families, often for years to come.

Mary's Little Prince brother moved Mom into a senior community, a decision Mary thought responsible. However, he refused to let Mom's priest visit, refused her last rites, and refused Mary's request for a funeral, burial, and memorial service. Little Prince simply decided Mom would be cremated. Mary knew this decision to be contrary to Mom's religious history and beliefs, but there was nothing she could do.

Mary's brother's attitude reflects meanness—and God only knows the unfinished emotional business with Mom and siblings. It's hard to overcome mean. The brother is a poisonous person. There is no antidote. But it is still hard for caring people to throw up their hands and give up on family, even if they are deadly.

Sibling rivalry shows up in many ways. I saw one daughter slap another daughter standing over their mother's casket over whether the jewelry around the loved one's neck should be buried with her or kept as a remembrance. Dysfunction can arise when one sibling has formal authority for a loved one and others have day-to-day management of care. Sibling rivalry starts early and ends late in life. These relationships were described to me as, "I feel like I have a high voltage wire. I can't hold on, and I can't let go." There are three basic strategies to mitigate its effects on the entire family. One is to get counseling. A second is to let go of the high voltage wire: simply surrender. The third strategy is time. Time, distance, and subsequent events soften rivalries. People can gain wisdom and perspective with time. It is hard to stop fighting, but most sibling rivalry has deep and dark roots that simply can't be changed. So, let it go! Remember: "Never try to teach a pig to sing. You waste your time and annoy the pig."

Destructive *sibling rivalry* can last a lifetime.

BARRIER #8—DENIAL: "The Naked Truth"

Another great Wesley Woods board member, the late Palacia Seaman, told the story of a friend's encounter with the naked truth. Her friend was married to a globe-trotting executive whose mother lived with them. There had apparently been long-standing tension between the mom and daughter-in-law.

The daughter-in-law had noticed increased signs of mental impairment, but every time she brought it up to her husband, he dismissed her concerns. He accused his wife of trying to get Mom out of their home and often said to her, "You never liked my mom anyway! She's fine!" Mom was always on her best behavior when her son was in town.

One evening, the son and daughter-in-law hosted what I would call a three-fork dinner party for the husband's boss, spouse, and other corporate executives. As the occasion shifted from cocktail hour to seating for dinner, the boss's wife asked the hostess where the powder room was. Hostess pointed her to the door leading to the bathroom corridor. All were surprised when boss's wife opened the door to find Mom standing on the other side, stark naked in the hallway. Only then did the son admit his mom had a problem.

Most often, the signs and symptoms are not as dramatic as a naked relative. Over the holidays the out-of-town family notices changes that those in town don't see because of the subtleties of them. Not remembering the names of grandchildren. Pots left on a hot stove. A fall in the parking lot at the pharmacy. A smoke alarm or police call. A fender bender. Unkempt appearance of home or person. Unexplained disappearance of assets like bank withdrawals or loss of silverware. Spoiled food in the refrigerator. Medications obviously not well managed. Reduced interest in activities that previously brought pleasure.

Usually something triggers the need to talk about aging and its inevitabilities. The questions become: Who speaks up? What triggers the conversation? Until someone does so, denial is the powerful suppressive dynamic that inhibits intervention before someone gets hurt.

Why is denial so powerful? One, no one really wants to believe their loved ones have a problem, especially when it comes to losing one's mind or losing functional abilities that put independence at risk. And no one wants to watch their parents grow old. And no one wants to admit it can—and will—happen to us.

Two, there are unresolved sibling and/or parental relationship issues that are skeletons too painful to risk their letting out of the closet. There is shame in disclosing Uncle Gene's condition.

Three, admitting there are health problems creates new work in otherwise busy lives. After all, someone has to broach the subject with Mom or Dad. Someone has to take them to the doctor for the tests involved. Someone has to organize and orchestrate a plan of action to make sure Mom or Dad can safely stay at home or choose an institutional setting. Caregiving is full-time work, whether done by one individual family member or shared.

Four, caregiving costs money. The costs of caregiving borne by seniors and their loved ones far exceed taxpayer money spent through public programs like Medicaid. Sometimes families have to choose between private school tuition for kids or better, more expensive, nursing home care for parents.

Five, caregiving creates additional stress on caregivers and more complicated relationship dynamics. Caregiving stress makes existing personal health and relationship conflicts erupt at new levels. Denial can be so powerful that it can lead loved ones to passively allow events to dictate intervention. "If Mom or Dad has an auto accident or breaks a hip, *then* we will intervene," they tell themselves. And often, *denial* whispers in their ear that they are protecting Mom or Dad's "dignity" and "independence" as the rationale for doing nothing. But there is nothing that protects against the guilt of knowing that irreparable harm has come to someone because *you* didn't want to face a naked truth.

I define *denial* as the art of fooling oneself for selfish purposes. It is perhaps the *most* powerful barrier to the confronting of problems associated with aging.

BARRIER #9—INADEQUATE PLANNING: "The Fortune on the Table"

The pastor at a large church called about Mr. and Mrs. Fewell, who had called him for help. Mr. Fewell was familiar with Wesley Woods, where I worked, because of its Methodist affiliation. He wondered about the possibility of moving in. I agreed to pay the Fewells a visit since neither of them drove any longer.

The Fewells lived in a once prestigious neighborhood surrounding the legendary golfer Bobby Jones's home golf course, East Lake. But the area had become blighted and was one of the highest crime areas of Atlanta at that time.

The Fewells greeted me warmly. He was in a wheelchair but had his faculties. She was ambulatory but had that vacant smiling countenance of someone impaired. He invited me into their dining room. He offered me a chair, directed her to sit, and pulled his wheelchair up to an old oak table. On that table were several hundred thousand dollars in stocks, bonds, and cash.

Mr. Fewell got to the point: "Our health is failing. I have physical problems, and the wife is mentally confused. We have no family, so I need to provide for her after I'm gone. We shouldn't live alone any longer. I'm sure I'll go first. I'd like for you to take all this and guarantee that we'll both have a place to live the rest of our lives at Wesley Woods. And after we're gone, Wesley Woods can keep what's left."

I assured him that he and his wife had more than enough resources to last them the rest of their lives. Wesley Woods would be pleased to accept them as residents, though she might need special attention. However, I could not simply take the money. I recommended that he retain an attorney and establish a trust with an institution that could manage their resources. I told him that he could provide for Wesley Woods in his will if there were resources left when they died, but those decisions should be made between himself and his legal representative. He asked my help in finding a good lawyer. I knew of several and made a referral.

There was urgency, not for health reasons, but potential crime. I was aware that just a few weeks earlier, an elderly couple who were grandparents of a high school classmate had been robbed and murdered just a few doors down from the Fewells.

Fast forward a few weeks: I received word that Mrs. Fewell had moved into the Budd Terrace dementia program, but Mr. Fewell had died. But he did so knowing his wife would be cared for. Fast forward again a few years: I received word that Mrs. Fewell was running out of resources and would need charitable support, which the Wesley Woods Foundation provided. So, how did this situation go from a fortune on the dining room table to poverty in such a short amount of time? I still do not know. But what I found out was that there was a long-lost nephew who began to visit Mrs. Fewell. We can guess the rest of the story. Some people have a "woodwork" family that emerges at night like roaches. The "woodworkers" can be kinfolks, new friends who lavish attention on the Mrs. Fewells of the world, legitimate charities and illegitimate charlatans. But they have a nose for vulnerable people who have money. Had Mrs. Fewell not wound up living in an organization with ethical standards and a charitable program, she could have been discharged to the nearest available Medicaid nursing home bed and would have become even more of a lost soul than she was.

There are millions of situations like the Fewell's. While some are well-off like Mrs. Fewell, others are poor people who are imprisoned in a family unit because their meager Social Security checks are needed to underwrite family expenses. Many of these people need to be in a nursing home like Mrs. Fewell but are prevented by the "woodworkers" from living in one because they control the pension checks, which would otherwise be used to pay for care, as prescribed by law.

It is no secret that Americans don't plan for retirement adequately enough. Most are ignorant of the fact that there are significant out-of-pocket health and long-term care expenses not covered by government or private insurance. On top of that exposure, too few of us set aside money every month for retirement.

Alberta was chief housekeeper at Wesley Woods. She had been an employee of Emory and Wesley Woods all her adult life. She came to see me to announce her retirement, at a relatively young age. Much of her career in housekeeping compensated her at near minimum-wage level, so I asked her why retire now and how she planned to make ends meet financially. She responded that she had plans to travel and spend more time on things she enjoyed while she was relatively young and healthy. As to making ends meet, Alberta grinned and told me she'd been maximizing the retirement plan that Emory and Wesley Woods offered over the years and had accumulated several hundred thousand dollars in corpus. That, plus Social Security and no major debt, left her very comfortable. Alberta planned well, managed well, sought professional help, and disciplined herself to be comfortable.

There are two basic questions that each of us has a responsibility to answer, in writing, with an attorney, that express our choices far in advance of needing to make them. If these two questions are answered, significant problems for future generations are avoided:

Question 1: Who has the authority to pull the plug?

Question 2: Who has the authority to manage the money?

Without clarity on these fundamentals, there is high disaster potential.

A major barrier to aging successfully is *poor planning!*

There is one overriding intervention that mitigates against the above nine barriers: open communication, or, as I call it, "the talk."

Every major stage of life precipitates the need for "the talk." Marriage, children, schooling, career planning, healthcare directives, where to live, financial planning. Many families involve all stakeholders in these major decision points by getting professional help and seeking advice from family and friends. But too many do not. When seniors can think through what their desires and choices are under predictable circumstances and draw their loved ones into those discussions through "the talk," life can end with few, if any, regrets. The possibility of dying at "a good old age" is exponentially more achievable. And when families see changes in the health and security of elderly loved ones, they need to say something. In today's security-conscious vernacular: "If you see something, say something." The regrets for not doing so are powerful.

So, let's talk about regrets.

11

The Endgame

"...grief but no regrets..."

I believe that regrets, or the lack thereof, are the most influential harbinger of bad or good health and of successful aging for the next two generations of family. As one woman told me in the midst of long-standing frustrations with her mother, "Here's my goal: The day after we put Mother in the ground, I want to look myself in the mirror and say, 'You've done the best you could do by her.'" Another said, "I want to be able to face my Maker and say, 'I've done the best I can.'" Or, as many have simply put it, "No regrets!"

A family admitted their mother to the Wesley Woods neuropsychiatric unit for severe behavioral management problems. The daughters were in desperate need of rest, a vacation. At the first care conference, the daughters complained that their mother was still irascible and angry. They had hoped that with professional care their mother would "get well." In fact, they were looking for our staff to help create the ideal mother they had always longed for, which, of course, could never happen.

Gently, the staff pointed out the family's unrealistic expectations. A few days later, the daughters and their husbands met with the mother's physician. A son-in-law spokesman explained to the doctor that they had thought about their expectations. They realized that the women's mother had been a mean, difficult person all her life. She had been a terrible mother. No one in the family liked her. They were all experiencing huge, long-standing regrets about a mother they never had. But the two couples had decided that it was their responsibility to make sure the mother had the care she needed and they would do the best by her that they could. They asked the doctor, "Help us do the right thing so we can live with ourselves after she's gone."

In contrast, recently a dear friend had to admit his father to hospice. The father had faced several years of losses: wife, health, financial resources, theft of precious objects by trusted in-home companions. My friend and his wife traveled to see him as he lay on his deathbed, the picture of a brand-new great-granddaughter in hand. My friend wrote, "Dad died as we were on the way back to the airport this a.m., so we were lucky to share with him the photo of his new great-granddaughter and hear him talk about how rich his life had been." Since the father felt his life had been worthwhile, his death left the family with grief but no regrets.

It is important to distinguish between regrets and grief. Grief expresses the sentiment that you deeply miss someone or something very important, and it really hurts. "Parting is such sweet sorrow," as Shakespeare put it. It means you miss the person and mourn the loss. Regrets, however, mean that there is unfinished business: sentiments not expressed, conflicts unresolved for too long, acts of kindness not done, acts for which there has been no apology. Regrets leave the remaining family with guilt and anger that can even affect future generations. Mental and physical illness result from regrets.

There are different types of regrets. *Commission* regrets are acts of intentional or unintentional hurts we cause others. Often these regrets take the form of mean things we say that cannot be taken back or apologized for. Earlier, I spoke of a relative who had an argument filled with hateful rhetoric. Then, his sudden death a few days later left his son with years of addiction. Had my friend lived longer, reconciliation would have been likely, but it was now impossible.

Omission regrets are largely woulda, shoulda, coulda neglectful nonaction. "If only" are the key words that signal omissions. I regret not keeping up with Ain Nettie and Unca Clarence. As an old friend said to me when in the midst of angst over something I could no longer do anything about, "Well, if a frog had wings, it wouldn't bump its ass jumping over a log, would it?" Omission regrets are a dark and endless pit of guilt and shame unless we learn to forgive ourselves and make amends by doing for others what we did not do for a loved one. And by sometimes visiting a gravesite and expressing them out loud over the grave.

Failure causes regret. Trying new things in life inevitably generates failure because not everything we attempt is successful. We teach our children to either try again or try something new. Baseball legend Hank Aaron said, "You make the Hall of Fame batting one for three."

Relationship failures are risky. Many people try time and again at relationship healing only to be hurt again and again, often by the same person. People who won't accept overtures or apology and reconciliation are often poisonous. So, leave them alone. Relationship failure extremes can create a cycle of abuse. The more my mother tried to create harmony with her poisonous sister, Olivia, the more emotionally battered she became until my father put his foot down about any further contact. But Mother always regretted failing at it.

Cowardice creates regrets. Sometimes we experience well-deserved self-blame and the blame of others because we make no attempt to extend a helping hand or empathetic ear. Often the causes of cowardice are our own self-absorption, denial, or fear about the health conditions of the other person, as if every health problem were contagious. There is no age-related health problem without attendant side effects that are pretty to look at or easy to smell.

I remember visiting with a young woman dying of cancer at Emory Hospital during my chaplain CPE internship. It was a Saturday evening. As I entered the room, the smell of Nair (a popular hair removal product of the time) accented the fact that she was dressed in a pink nightgown and wore makeup. She was a newlywed, married to her high school sweetheart. There were pictures on her bedside stand of him in his football uniform and her in her cheerleader outfit. They married right after high school, followed soon thereafter by her cancer.

I commented on how pretty she looked and offered that she must be expecting her husband, so I would only stay a minute or two. Yes, she was hopeful that he would come, but she said he had only visited once or twice during her long stay at Emory. (At the time, there were no hospice programs to help her stay at home.) "He can't bear to see me like this," she said. "I feel like I'm in a deep well. My husband doesn't visit at all. My parents visit but they try to cheer me up and pray for me. The nurses pretend I don't have cancer. You're about the only one who just stops at the top of the well and listens to me and talks."

Cowardice often carries lasting, self-inflicted wounds. I have wondered what happened to that young husband who may or may not have had access to help that would coach him through one of life's most difficult situations: loss of a spouse, especially at such a young age. Make yourself smell the Nair in people you love and talk about it.

Circumstantial regrets are created by bad timing, busy lives, human error, and logistical circumstances. We can't always be at the bedside or visit face-to-face at crucial times. We don't always say the right thing or give the best advice. Kay wasn't at Mama's bedside, but she had expressed her love to her mother. Our loved ones in crisis may not always be the relationship priority because of others in our lives who are even more important. So, it isn't our fault when we get that phone call that Grandma has died. Hopefully, the last call or visit had a happy ending.

Finally, there are *Wonder Woman* or *Superman* regrets. Competent people often believe they can do it all and have it all. They tell themselves, "If I were really an adequate daughter [or mother or wife], I could [fix this situation, those people]." One of the Dutiful Daughters had Wonder Woman expectations of herself that just would not totally leave her. Stress for Wonder Woman and Superman is inevitable, as are stress-related illnesses. This is the place for spouse, children, and friends to ground us in reality and pitch in to help. It sounds like this: "Mama, this situation can't be fixed." Or, "Dad, I'll take Grandpa to the doctor." Or, "We're going to counseling to help us keep this in perspective." Marilyn's daughter pitched in when it was obvious Marilyn was on emotional overload. The Dutiful Daughters supported each other regularly.

Wonder Woman and Superman often become "lightning rod" children. As they take on more and more caregiving responsibilities, other siblings are happy to back away, which they believe gives them the right to complain about what is or isn't being done for Mom. Ironically, the lightning rod children are the strong ones, often in the guise of a beleaguered demeanor. The emotional storm clouds of regret, grief, anger, and guilt combine to generate electricity on the lightning rod caregiving. Often, once a lightning rod person understands the dynamic, they can more easily let the lightning go harmlessly to ground. But that is hard to do. When caregivers don't have a ground wire through various kinds of help, it leads to the two most difficult feelings that result. The first is the self-imposed judgment that they should have done *more* for Mom. Of course, this has been drilled into them by other relatives who have stood in judgment on the sidelines.

Sometimes that feeling fades with reflection and reassurance from other family and friends. I remember a daughter who came up to me in a restaurant a few years after her mother's death in the Wesley Woods nursing home. While her mother lived there for an extended period of time, the daughter stayed with her mother eight to twelve hours a day. She took copious notes of what staff had done or had not done for her mother. She reported those regularly to our nurse leadership and me. Continuous complaints and palpable hostility.

At the restaurant, however, she reintroduced herself, asked if I remembered her. "Of course. How could I forget?" I responded. She smiled. Then, "I owe you an apology. Looking back, I know I was difficult. I hadn't realized how crazy I acted until a close neighbor recently had to put her mother in a nursing home. She started coming by my house every day for a cup of coffee before she went to the nursing home to spend all day. She went over her daily litany of complaints about the care. She was so angry about her mother's condition and was blaming the staff. I saw myself in her. Then I said to her, 'You know, I've been exactly where you are and nearly drove myself crazy, and the staff at Wesley Woods as well. I'm sure they are doing the best they can, but they can't change your mother's overall condition. And if you keep this up, you'll drive yourself crazy. I recommend you visit less often and let the staff do their jobs.' So, Mr. Minnix, I am sorry. Everybody was doing the best they could, including me." Apology accepted.

The second major realization is that no matter how much you love someone with an extended caregiving need, no matter how much you will miss them with the good times, and no matter how good you feel about the caregiving job you did, part of you feels *relief* that it's over. There is often shame for feeling this way. If admitted out loud, there is the risk of blame by those who have their own conflicts about aging parents, dying, disability, and death. But the emotional reality is that people who linger uncomfortably are out of their misery when they die, which we can accept. And the other part of the emotional package is that we are out of *our* misery with the caregiving saga. Kay understood this and understood her own mother's prayer to die sooner.

Sometimes regrets are unavoidable because personalities and circumstances make it impossible to deal with them. I have often told people steeped in the sickness of regret that such relationship fissures can only be healed in the next world, in God's hands. The question then becomes: Can you forgive *yourself* for your own imperfections and motives, including your inability to change another person? The Bible says God forgives and then he forgets. Our problem is that we humans have trouble with both.

Turds-in-the-punchbowl people can't forgive others and can't forgive themselves. So, at the time of death, for a family to honestly say, "I've done the best I know how to do," and for an older person to be able to tell the family that life has been "rich," these are the foundations for the "good old age" and death without regrets. The term "rest in peace" takes on powerful meaning at the graveside when we can say we have few, if any, regrets, that we will miss the good times, and that we will let ourselves feel relief that this chapter of our lives is over: the ultimate earthly hallowed ground that awaits us all someday.

Retirement

"...thar he goes..."

My decision to retire in 2015 at the age of sixty-eight prompted reflection about my own aging. If I recall a particular *Monday Night Football* broadcast in its early days, the color commentators were the inimitable Howard Cosell and the Folksy Don Meredith, a retired quarterback of the Dallas Cowboys. Frank Gifford, retired pro player, added his smooth style of play-by-play.

On one play, the quarterback scrambled out of bounds to avoid a collision with an oncoming linebacker. Cosell condemned what he perceived to be the cowardice of that quarterback in not taking on the linebacker. Don Meredith responded in his Texas drawl, "Howard, I been where that boy's been. And believe me, it's better to say, 'Thar he goes,' rather than 'Thar he lays.'"

Sports metaphors can be trite, but this one illustrates that we have the option of exiting the game artfully or continuing to confront the daily hits of our profession to our detriment and the detriment of our "team." Yet retirement is a big deal for many because it can either extend quality life in a new phase or kill us.

Baby boomers are turning sixty-five at the rate of ten thousand per day. That age had become identified as the age to retire, though it has been raised to age seventy now, and both those numbers are arbitrary. Otto von Bismark of Germany established sixty-five as retirement age to make employment room for younger people. "Retirement at sixty-five is ridiculous," George Burns, the comedian who worked until he was ninety-eight, said. "When I was sixty-five, I still had pimples." (Johnny Carson also asked Burns on *The Tonight Show* when the last time was that he had sex. He simply and subtly looked down and glanced at his watch. The audience and Carson came apart at the seams.) Retirement at sixty-five or seventy is still an arbitrary number.

Yet, aging is eventually accompanied by decline in physical ability, judgment, and mental acuity. In spite of oneself, we can be contributors to society well into what is now considered "retirement age." As one country-western singer puts it, "I'm not as good as I once was. But I'm as good once as I ever was."

I spoke at a board of trustees meeting of a Lutheran senior community in Iowa. I asked each board member to introduce themselves with what their "day job" was and why they served on this board. One member responded, "Well, I'm retired." I asked him how much time he spent on this board, plus other causes he supported. "I was a corporate executive for many years. I have a farm that I really enjoy. I serve on this board. And the Lutheran college next to us. I'm on the hospital board. I'm active in my church. And I'm president of my civic club...Come to think of it, I guess I would define retirement as getting up every day and doing what I damn well please!"

I believe "retirement" will become an antiquated term soon. Perhaps it will be replaced with "do-damner." That concept resonates with me. It is exactly what I do now, for the most part. But it hasn't been easy getting there *emotionally*.

As I entered my sixties, I intellectualized about retirement. It was all around me in my work. I saw friends and colleagues who seemed to have done it really well, and others who had not. I was particularly tuned in to CEOs since I had been one for so long. In addition, a survey of LeadingAge CEOs, most of whom were about the same age as me, said that the thing that kept them up at night most was where the next generation of leaders was coming from, since a significant percentage of us would be retiring within the next decade. So, LeadingAge developed a Leadership Academy for emerging leaders and also emphasized succession planning for boards of directors and CEOs like myself. Over six hundred people have completed the academy, and formal succession plans are increasingly becoming important board policy for the institution.

As I passed the age-sixty-five milestone, more people would ask when I planned to "hang it up." I loved my work, so I deflected the topic with flip responses like, "I plan to get out a year before you guys get tired of me." Or, "You'll know when you read my obit that says I was found slumped over my desk." I received many ego strokes from LeadingAge colleagues who inadvertently reinforced my delusion that I could do the job indefinitely, and even that I was indispensable. Fortunately, I am married to Kathleen, a woman who kept my ego from becoming too inflated and my feet grounded in reality. I heard about a successful business leader who had achieved some noteworthy milestone and asked his wife, "Honey, do you know how many truly great men there are in our business today?" She responded, "One less than you think."

Well-thought-out corporate CEO succession plans guard against ego and indispensability by setting a predetermined age, announcing a search or less apparent process, providing for a six- to twelve-month transition, and giving the member a good send-off. The incumbent then steps out of the way with a clean break.

When I was CEO of Wesley Woods, the board decided to craft a succession plan before there was a need for one. One of our wise trustees, Billy Warren, introduced the topic to the board by looking at me and saying, "A succession plan is simply this: Larry, if you leave us, or God forbid, get hit by a bus, our board's job is to appoint a search committee to have someone replace you within six months who, in spite of what a great job you do, can do it better than you did." I have noticed that those organizations that have formal plans along the lines of Billy's advice seem to have healthy transitions and bright futures. Organizations have difficulty when there is no plan or when their CEOs face retirement but take years to do it, while talking about it incessantly.

I remember a pointed interchange with a CEO I had known for years whose organization was declining because of his lack of energetic leadership as he aged. He said to me, "I just don't enjoy it much anymore. I don't have the energy for it." I asked him why he didn't retire, and he said, "I can't financially; I don't know what I'd do. And I enjoy the status." He was stuck, and so was his organization.

I have seen "never can say good-bye" CEOs whose succession plan is more focused on massaging their egos than planning for the organization's future leadership. This often leads to the turnover of other executive staff, board conflict and indecisiveness about the organization's strategic plan, and uncertainty among donors and business supporters. Some say they still feel great at their age, so why have a plan until "the time comes," whenever that is. These colleagues don't realize that they often become an embarrassment to themselves. Professional sports are littered with athletes whose teams retire them, yet they decide to sign up another season or two because they think they can still play, only to have their own records diminish and have the commentators say frequently that "they've lost a step or two."

So, my advice: get out on top. Sliding to the bottom isn't pretty.

The LeadingAge board and I had targeted my retirement at seventy. There was a succession plan in place. The rationale for seventy was strategic for LeadingAge. That would be the year a new White House would be in place, along with a new Congress. This meant that my successor would have the opportunity to forge relationships with the new bodies politic in the time period where policy direction is often set for the next several years. When the board and I decided this timetable, I was still midsixties. Age seventy seemed far away. I denied the reality of it except for financial planning. But the Wesley Woods and LeadingAge retirement plans were generous, and I maximized my contribution to them. I took a lesson from Alberta's playbook.

To foreshadow, a friend sent me a Jewish proverb: "We plan. God laughs." My scenario was disrupted by two events.

My wife, Kathleen, who has managed a chronic illness for all her adult life, experienced a new level of symptoms that could limit her physical abilities, energy, and vision. Our ideal plan included a bucket list of trips, including frequent jaunts to the West Coast to enjoy a new granddaughter there. (Now there are additional twins there and two granddaughters here in Atlanta.) Suddenly, those dreams were at risk.

The second event involved our chief operating officer at LeadingAge, Katie Smith Sloan. I hired her a decade earlier when I went to Washington. She is tops: best executive hire I ever made. I thought of her as my successor at LeadingAge, though we rarely discussed it, because the succession plan called for a national search to assure all LeadingAge stakeholders that the board had secured the best possible person. Katie disclosed to me that she had a tempting CEO opportunity in Washington. I asked about her thoughts on being my successor. She still contemplated the possibility, and she knew the succession plan timetable meant retirement for me was a few years out. So, I faced a double dilemma: Do I bow out early to maximize time with my wife? Better to say we did fulfilling things while we were at our healthiest than that I regretted not retiring and wishing I had. Do I let the organization risk losing a top executive? To paraphrase Don Meredith, it would be better to say, "Here she stays," rather than "Thar she goes."

I explained the situation to the LeadingAge chair, Dave Gehm of Lutheran Homes of Michigan and chair-elect Kathryn Roberts of Ecumen in Minnesota. Because of Kathleen's health scare and the decision Katie might make about another CEO position, I recommended to Dave that the board announce my retirement, that Katie be named heir apparent, and that she be installed as the LeadingAge CEO by the end of 2014. The board stuck to the succession plan, assured Katie she would be strongly considered if she applied, and thereby maintained an orderly change based on time-tested principles of corporate transition. Katie competed and succeeded. I was given the best send-off imaginable. *And* I got out of the way.

But the truth is, I was terrified to retire. Kathleen and I had not dealt with questions like: What will I do every day? Will I have enough money? What happens when I become ill or disabled? Where should I live and under what circumstances? Will my wife and I be able to tolerate each other's company all day? A friend avoided retirement even at the age of seventy because he said that he and his wife vowed, "For better or worse, but not for lunch." Another quipped, "Twice as much husband for half the income."

When I decided to retire, I panicked. I had worked since I was ten. I sold Coca-Colas and blackberries. I mowed lawns, painted windows, and spread pine straw. Through high school and college, my parents paid the basics of my education, and I earned money for my social life. My parents both worked. We were lower middle class. Daddy returned from World War II and drifted a while. He was a good salesman, but his lack of a college education was limiting. Once when he was without a job, I heard him pleading with a potential employer on the phone, "Look man, I can sell horseshit to filling stations! Just give me a chance!"

Mother went to work for local government. It was steady and had benefits, but when I was in my early teen years, she and Daddy fell down on their luck. She had surgery not covered by any insurance, and he had no paycheck. I knew nothing of their financial plight. I found out years later that the clock radio I wanted for Christmas was acquired by generous neighbors who pooled their Green Stamps. (For younger generations, Green Stamps were an early version of rewards points, but they were dispensed at grocery stores.)

Daddy finally found a sales position, and Mother rose in the ranks of the county tax office. Together their incomes paid my college tuition beyond the scholarships I received. And I worked at Sears, Macy's, and a psychiatric facility in order to pay for my social life. No matter our financial struggles, we always found a welcome at our church. We had a great youth program. It was around a youth retreat campfire at age fifteen that I first heard my calling to the ministry. It was the calling that eventually led me to senior service through Wesley Woods.

I played trumpet in high school band. And youth baseball. I had many friends. And I had a 1953 Plymouth with a dent in the side that wasn't repaired because of the money and because my parents thought it a good reminder of the importance of paying attention when I drove. "The Blue Bomb" had no radio, no heater, and periodic brake failure. When I became old enough to drive it to high school, I parked it on a hill to "kick it off" by jumping the clutch after building up some speed.

Yes, I had a no-frills childhood, but I had everything that made life worthwhile at that age and a thorough grounding in a strong work ethic. But I had no role modeling for what is now called "work-life balance." My family took only a couple of vacations. One to the Great Smoky Mountains. The other to Parrot Jungle in Florida. Neither was much fun. Couldn't wait to get home to friends and church. The best vacations I remember were at Ain Nettie and Unca Clarence's, where I could play in the woods, fish, and only bathe on Saturday before church the next day.

Not knowing how to break from work caught up with me in the early years of marriage. When Kathleen and I went out of town, I obsessed about work. After our two sons came along, she bought a timeshare in North Carolina for a week in the summer. She said she'd take the boys and hoped I'd join them, but if I needed more time alone to work, I'd have that choice. I went! The first couple of years, I carried my briefcase and worked by phone. Gradually, I learned to leave the briefcase behind. Friends noticed how my pre-occupation with my job was affecting my wife's happiness. I was startled when one of them asked, "Since you are cheating on your wife with work, can I have an affair with her?" He said it in jest, but the question sobered me up about the personal toll my job was taking on my family.

Daddy, the unexpressive and emotionally isolated Archie Bunker, noticed my obsession with work during a particularly intense time at Wesley Woods. At the kitchen table and, out of the blue, Daddy ventured, "I'm gonna give you some advice, son." (This had *never* happened before.) He proceeded, "Don't ever marry a company. I did. It's not good for your family. And I've regretted it." He got up and went into the den to watch the Braves. Enough said. Yet it said all.

I had two big fears about retirement: the "Bear Bryant Syndrome" and the "Jimmy Carter Syndrome." Bear Bryant, the legendary coach of the Alabama Crimson Tide, died one month after retiring. And Jimmy Carter fought depression, successfully, I may add, for many months after he lost his bid for a second presidential term.

I did not know Bear Bryant. But I did preach at Jimmy Carter's church after he gave one of his very popular Sunday School lessons. This came about because his presidential center was part of Emory University, as was Wesley Woods, where I was CEO. He and Rosalynn were interested in Alzheimer's and caregiving. A breakfast at the Carter Center led to an invitation to visit President Carter at their home in Plains, Georgia, to explore ideas of mutual interest.

During the tour of the Carter home place, we chatted in his office, the Jimmy Carter man cave in today's vernacular. His phone rang. He hung up after a short conversation. "Forgive the interruption," he said. "That was my publisher. My book is out today. I have a copy for you." And he began to inscribe it. "It's called *The Virtues of Aging*. It's about the transition Rosalynn and I made after the White House." I asked him what that was like. "It was difficult. We became depressed and got help with it. Imagine that one day you are *the* most powerful person in the world, and the next day your phone doesn't ring. That's a big adjustment."

The "Bear Bryant Syndrome" and the "Jimmy Carter Syndrome" caused me to fear dying or depression after retirement. I especially feared this since I had planned nothing else to *do*. I sought advice. Some told me to think of a hobby or new venture before retiring and transition into it. "Don't let go of the trapeze until you know that the next platform or rung of the trapeze is in place." Others suggested consulting. Interim CEO work. Arts and crafts. Paid speaker. Run for office.

Still others said retire, rest, adjust to a new daily routine, and see what comes my way. The person who helped me sort through these two alternatives was Kathleen Anderson, longtime friend and CEO of Goodwin House in Alexandria, Virginia. She asked me how I wanted to finish my tenure at LeadingAge after fifteen years as CEO. Many colleagues and friends had advised me to coast the last few months. Take it easy. Taper off. Knock off early. Delegate trips, speaking requests. But Kathleen helped me see two things: One is that I wanted to finish strong. In fact, I saw my last months as a leg in a relay race. For fifteen years, I had had the baton, and I planned to be running hard when I passed it off to my successor. And they better be running hard when they took it from me. No, I couldn't ease off and back out slowly.

Two, Kathleen Anderson helped me see that what I would do next would be revealed to me, just like my original calling. Don't worry about what to do next. Just enjoy the last months of a successful career and trust my calling.

What a relief! I was able to speak to my biggest fears as I faced retirement: isolation, irrelevance, and impotence. I need not be the victim of any of them. The panic about the decision went away. My wife was relieved but skeptical. She was vigilant about boredom, depression, or ill health. I found she was right about one thing. I was far wearier than I knew. I had been repressing exhaustion for a while. I was tired of schlepping through airports and had become cynical about Washington gridlock. My family encouraged me to write this book: a collection of stories about real people and successful life lessons about aging.

Ill health did sneak up on me in early 2017, a year after retiring. I thought I was having (shall we say) a "Preparation H problem," which devolved into an abscess requiring five surgeries and a temporary ostomy. (Thankfully, I am now reconnected and on the mend.) Awaiting my future calling of prestigious board appointments laced with trips and grandkids suddenly turned into two hospital stays and months of recovery. I had taken very few sick days during my entire forty-five-year career, only to become a Medicare patient for several weeks in the hospital. The goal of a trip to Fiji turned into three laps around the nurses' station, IV pole in tow. I suddenly was a recipient of health delivery programs I had worked hard to support. I received great care and had minimal financial stress thanks to Medicare and supplemental insurance. My wife's limited supply of energy to finish a book she had meticulously researched for several years was redirected to caregiving. She was really good at it but sacrificed herself in the process.

We have come out of 2017 with better focus on priorities, less patience with people and groups who like to complain or meet for the sake of accomplishing nothing. We took a bucket-list-trip tour of the Christmas markets of Prague and Vienna; we have had more time with family. We are involved in causes that effect change. And we have concentrated on our beautiful home, which my wife has restored.

We are "do-damners." Nothing else matters but family, friends, good causes, fun trips, and single malt scotch on our front porch or back patio. When confronted with limitations and mortality, it is amazing how clearly you can focus on things that *really* matter and just give deep pleasure.

So, my advice about approaching retirement is:

1. Make a plan for yourself and your organization.

2. Get out at the top of your game.

3. Announce a date, and stick to it.

4. Let your colleagues celebrate you, and bask in it.

5. Make a clean break, and get the hell out of the way of your successor.

6. And, finally, shut up about it until just a few months before it occurs.

Bottom line for emergency do-damners: Retire. Rest. Renew. Reengage.

Those Places

"...this place inspires optimism..."

"Promise me you'll never put me in one of 'those places,'" is a refrain sung by many seniors as they and an adult child pass by a senior community. Often it is a promise that cannot be kept. There are health and safety concerns that inevitably arise that cannot be managed at home within the family budget. This chapter is mostly technical in defining the senior living options available in most communities.

My wife and I were invited to a neighborhood dinner party in Alexandria, Virginia. Like us, the other guests were baby boomers. The other couples knew each other, and one asked Peter how his elderly mother was doing. He responded that she had been through a difficult time with health problems but had remained in her home nearby, where she became increasingly depressed and more demanding of Peter and his wife.

At wits' end, Peter inquired about Goodwin House, an Episco-palian-sponsored continuing care retirement community (CCRC), "one of those places," in Alexandria. (Increasingly, CCRCs are referred to as life plan communities.) He and his wife twisted his mother's arm to consider it and move in. He then reported gleefully that his mother was doing great. She had found old friends, had made new ones, had participated in various events and activities, and was enjoying the food. He went on to say that she was no longer depressed and hardly had time for him because she was so busy. His mother had moved into the independent living part of Goodwin House, but other levels of care were available there if she ever needed them.

I recall that Peter used the term "transformed" when reflecting on the impact Goodwin House had when contrasting his mother's life in recent months. A vibrant, healthy senior community, regardless of size and scope of services, *should* be life-enhancing and, yes, transformative. In fact, several LeadingAge senior community organizations like Eskaton in California, Kendal scattered throughout the mid-Atlantic region, and National Church Residences located in thirty states have mission statements that indicate their aim is to transform the aging experience that so many people dread.

So, the issue is, how do consumers know "transformative," high-quality senior living options that meet specific needs when and if the time comes, and how does the entire concerned family have peace of mind about the decision made? Affordable quality for senior consumers, peace of mind for the family, no regrets later. Those are the goals, and if achieved, are often personally transformative.

Goodwin House could be considered a near-idyllic prototype of a senior community. But there are other options less comprehensive and expensive that achieve similar impact in the lives of those who live in them. Let's define "those places," who is likely to need them, and the financial implications of using them. Then, let's lay out stories about people who used them successfully in the next chapter.

For the sake of discussion, "senior communities" is an umbrella term for an array of services, from the recently emerging "village" concept to hospital-like postacute care and specialized care like hospice and geriatric evaluation units.

A brief definition of the generic levels from the least to the most intensive:

VILLAGE: A neighborhood where residents have grown old together and want to stay in their homes through an organized approach to contract services like in-home care, home maintenance, transportation. Villages hire a concierge to orchestrate service delivery when needed. The concierge is usually an experienced social worker or nurse. Neighborhood residents share the cost through agreed-upon fees or dues. There are now hundreds of "villages" in various stages of development across the country.

SENIOR HOUSING: Specially designed senior housing with orchestration of services for older people who are still independent yet want the safety and security of a community. Senior housing has features like emergency call alarms, activity space, dining rooms, fitness room, and wellness clinic, where a nurse can monitor vital signs and see that transitions to and from a hospital are coordinated. The housing community may hire a nurse to oversee these services, or a local health system may provide the nurse to assure quality and continuity to avoid unnecessary hospitalization. These senior housing communities are often rental, with a sliding scale through government subsidy. But there are ownership models like cooperatives that offer service amenities, especially dining and housekeeping.

Increasingly, senior housing communities have a floor of personal and housekeeping care or assisted living, as the needs of an individual resident changes, or if one member of a couple needs twenty-four-seven monitoring because of dementia. The definition and licensing of these communities or floors may vary in name and regulatory oversight, depending on state law. Most of these communities have long waiting lists: ten people or more for every unit occupied.

ASSISTED LIVING (AL): ALs are generally for people who may not need a nursing home but cannot stay at home or with family. They are popular with the public because of the décor, quality of dining, other amenities, and private accommodations for each resident. Assisted living has twenty-four-hour watchful oversight and assistance with dressing, bathing, and medication management. Most have memory care units. Assisted living is also popular because it is *not* a nursing home. AL is largely self-pay and is dominated by for-profit companies that enjoy generous bottom lines at consumer expense. It has also battled consumer experiences of nondelivery, of not meeting expectations around the definition of "assisted." As one expert said, "Assisted living is often a lot of sizzle but not much steak."

Few standards govern assisted living. There are now so many AL communities across the country that government inspection and oversight is impossible and unaffordable. The AL sector is working on the development of self-regulating peer-review standards. It remains to be seen whether those standards will be widely operationalized and whether they will be effective. But for many families who have promised to "never put Mama in a nursing home," they are a convenient port in a storm.

NURSING HOME (NH): Well-defined and highly regulated communities that care for people who need physician oversight, twenty-four-seven professional nursing management, and compassionate, well-trained personal attention by direct care staff. NH residents frequently have multiple chronic conditions, often with a dementia overlay, and are on multiple medications.

A generation ago, NHs were largely a one-size-fits-all level of service, but they have evolved into two types of care. The first is now called postacute or subacute rehabilitation services, as a result of hip surgery or stroke. These postacute NHs usually have good relationships with local hospitals and sophisticated treatment capabilities with related quality metrics, which must be recorded and publicly reported. Every nursing home is inspected at least annually, and the results are made public for review on Medicare's website and in state inspection offices.

The most progressive of these postacute programs have features like a spa or health club, with single-room accommodations and the availability of professional nurses and therapists. Postacute care is covered by Medicare or private long-term insurance benefit up to defined limits. When someone's potential to get better plateaus, Medicare coverage ceases. Medicare rules pay for up to one hundred days, which few people receive. If a senior isn't ready to return home to a relatively independent lifestyle, families face alternative arrangements as described above, have their loved one move into the home of family, or go to a long-term nursing home described below.

The second type of NH that has evolved is long-term care. These residents require intensive professional nursing and direct care attention, along with creative approaches to quality of life programs like wheelchair exercises or video games or memory support group activities. Physical environments in progressive communities are evolving away from large, forty-to-fifty private and semiprivate rooms to "neighborhoods" a new model called "Green Houses" serving twelve to sixteen residents per house, each with a private accommodation. These environments are much more residential, with more restaurant-style dining, fireplaces, game rooms, and secure outdoor patios, walkways, and gardens. NHs are finally putting "home" into the nursing home. The role of technology is increasingly popular and important in helping residents not only have fun through games and art but in staying engaged with grandkids. Public dread of the *One Flew Over the Cuckoo's Nest* institutional image is fading. As one older man recovering from multiple health problems and family tragedy said of one of these new-era environments, "This place inspires optimism," an attitude he had not expected to have in his situation.

CONTINUUM SERVICES: A campus of senior services that offers three levels of service, including independent living, assisted living, and nursing home care. Continuums can be offered in separate buildings, like the Wesley Woods Campus in Atlanta, or they can be offered under one roof through distinct floors or units.

There are two types of continuum business models. One is an à-la-carte rental model where the resident pays for the level of service needed on a monthly or daily basis. The other is the continuing care retirement center (CCRC) or life plan model, which is financed through a combination of refundable entry fees and monthly service charge, depending on the needed level of service.

Life plan models are considered an insurance product in most every state because they guarantee access to higher levels of care when needed, avoiding the dreaded search for a nursing home bed in the event of hospitalization. Life plan models offer many advantages and are surprisingly economical and affordable when comparing the cost of living in them to the experience of living at home when in-home assistance is needed. Plus, the amenities offered like spas, transportation, wellness services, activities, and dining options, along with maintenance-free living, create the atmosphere that addresses risk factors associated with social isolation, poor nutrition, and fragmentation in care, all of which can be deadly. (More about these later.) A side benefit is that over 80 percent of life plan communities have not-for-profit sponsorships and ownerships; these almost invariably offer charitable assistance to residents who deplete their savings through no fault of their own.

There are thousands of senior housing and assisted living communities, fifteen thousand nursing homes, and two thousand life plan (CCRC) communities to choose from. There are numerous options available for seniors who are in the lower-middle-income to upper-income classes. There are too few options for seniors of modest means. Housing with government subsidies have long waiting lists, and Medicaid, which has its limits, is the only option for low-income seniors needing medical care.

The seniors most at risk for limited living arrangements are the middle-class poor, those people who have too much to qualify for Medicaid or rental assistance but not enough to pay out-of-pocket for care and services for any length of time. These seniors often turn to family for financial help to either move into a senior community or live directly with family. This adds stress to many families who have their own bills to pay and/or are assisting *their* children with tuition or have other expenses for grandchildren. In fact, the single biggest payor for senior services is not Uncle Sam, though the government's share of long-term care expenses is a sizeable taxpayer tab, but the personal out-of-pocket outlays of seniors and their families. Average projected outlay is well over $100,000 per individual but can be considerably more for conditions like Alzheimer's disease. Older women, whose pensions are less than those of men, will need more money because they live longer. Most people are unaware of their financial exposure. So, single women like Hilda (from chapter 5) will become increasingly common.

The "sandwich generation" is usually led by the daughter, who is often the designated family leader in addressing these complex challenges of "what to do with Mom." One such person came to see me in my nursing home administration days. Her mother was running out of money and wanted to apply for charitable funds assistance. She was a United Methodist and knew of our Methodist sponsorship at Wesley Woods. We had an active fund-raising plan called the Mother's Day Offering, and we had the benefit of annual foundation support to help us meet needs.

The daughter completed the application. Her mother had a very low income but owned several hundred acres of wheat fields in the Midwest, which meant she had assets in excess of Medicaid eligibility. I asked if she planned to liquidate the farmland for her mother's care. She became indignant and responded that the land had been in her family for generations and her mother planned to bequeath it to her grandchildren. The daughter also said that income from it was needed to help pay private school tuition.

We denied her request for assistance. She was angry, threatening to expose us to church leadership for not helping her mother, who was well deserving of it as a lifelong Methodist. I told her that she was really asking us to have donors subsidize her *family*, not her mother. Our mission was to help seniors, but before we ask donors to help, we expect the assets of seniors to be used first.

This is a microcosm of the family dilemma around the costs of aging. In today's senior services economic climate, needs are growing, government sources are becoming more constricted, and the middle-class poor (which is *most* people) do not have sufficient savings or personal insurance options to plan for inevitabilities. Who has several hundred thousands of dollars to pay for dementia services over a decade or more?

There were provisions in the Affordable Care Act (ACA) to create a voluntary national insurance pool to mitigate against the costs of senior care, but it was the first provision of the ACA to be stripped for political reasons, based on pressure from the long-term care insurance industry that saw it as a threat to their already dying insurance model of private long-term care. Since then, several studies have quantified emerging economic need and put forth options with estimated costs and premiums. Among those leading the effort to enact legislation to address this major and all-but-hidden issue are LeadingAge and the Bipartisan Policy Center, both based in Washington, and The SCAN Foundation, based in Southern California. All three have excellent information that is freely available.

What about the quality of the various options? The next chapter will address how people can recognize a good senior community when they see one, but measuring quality today is variable. There are few senior housing standards and no public oversight, except for Life Safety Code or local health department inspections of dining facilities. So, seniors and families will have to rely more on reputation, personal observation, and intuition.

Assisted living is struggling with self-regulated accreditation. Hopefully, the AL sector will establish and implement standards publicly sooner than later. But the biggest danger a senior in assisted living can be exposed to is staying in a place that looks appealing but is really not staffed to monitor and treat health conditions. Let the buyer beware and avoid being seduced by the sizzle.

Nursing homes are highly regulated, too much so, in fact. And some of the regulation is outdated compared to contemporary clinical practices. But nursing homes are regularly inspected, and there is public transparency about their track record. There are consistently excellent nursing homes, with few, if any, standards deficiencies. And there are those with consistently marginal or bad care track records. The Medicare website has these reports, as do state health agencies. Separating the wheat from the chaff is addressed in the next chapter. What is a healthy senior community, and how can consumers tell?

There is growing national interest in creating "age-friendly" and "dementia-friendly" towns and cities. My own hometown of Atlanta has a particularly visible interest in making our area more age friendly, with its Age-Friendly Atlanta Action Plan 2014–2016, approved by AARP (American Association of Retired Persons). Organizations like AARP, UsAgainstAlzheimer's, and LeadingAge are leaders in this emerging movement. These groups provide valuable information to consumers and to policymakers. It is particularly important that policymakers align changing needs with regulations and financing of services. At present, there are huge gaps and mismatches, leading to waste of money and unnecessary public and private expense.

So, how is community created for seniors and how can consumers know if they are healthy? Read on!

The Power of Organic and Planned Community

"…shiiiit, I don't need no Wesley Mountain Village…"

There are two kinds of senior communities: organic and planned. Here are examples of each and how they were selected by the consumers who chose each lifestyle embodied in them.

Wesley Woods developed several senior housing and life plan communities in Georgia. One of those developments was Wesley Mountain Village in the unlikely site of Blairsville, population 645 in the late 1970s, when it was built. The Village included 138 rental apartments and a few dozen cottages. Conventional market need studies reflected a need for no more than 38 apartments; yet the 138 units filled faster than any other Wesley Woods development at that time. It was the site of the thirteen marriages mentioned earlier.

The Village drew from seniors up north who were tired of

harsh winters and seniors from the south who had become too hot in summer. Most had originated from the area, wanted to "come back home" to the Appalachians, but had no way to do so until the Village was developed. It also drew from locals, many of whom lived in isolation up in the foothills. One such person was *not* Mr. Picklesheimer, though he taught me a great deal about what seniors need and want in senior living, inside or outside a senior community.

I met Mr. Picklesheimer at the community center in Blairsville. It was senior citizens' activity day. The center was a state-of-the-art chalet-style building surrounded by tennis courts, an Olympic standard swimming pool, basketball courts, a nine-hole golf course, and a deck with a 270-degree view of the beautiful Appalachian Mountains. I was invited there to make a pitch for Wesley Mountain Village in the predevelopment phase. The Village was right across the highway from the community center, so I could actually point to the location and extol the convenience of being close to the center's beautiful amenities.

Well over a hundred seniors were in attendance. There was mountain music, buck dancing, quilting and other crafts, and jawboning among friends on the deck, which is where I met Mr. Picklesheimer. I walked up to him and a few of his buddies. I wore a three-piece, pinstriped suit. (They looked at me funny. I never wore that suit to rural Appalachia again.) I introduced myself, passed out a Wesley Mountain Village brochure, pointed to the convenient location, and asked, flashing an Elmer Gantry/Burt Lancaster smile, "Anybody interested? You can sign up today to hold your place."

Silence…then from one of the group, "Picklesheimer's my name, young feller." He then lifted a paper coffee cup to one side of his mouth, spit his snuff (smokeless tobacco, for the uninitiated) residue into it, as he did every few words in his response to my inquiry about interest. His lower lip and right cheek swelled with the presence of it, and the cracks around his mouth dripped with what didn't make it into the cup. He began…slowly, "You know where the Widder [southern for widow] Jones's place is on the other side of town?" He spit. I wasn't familiar. "Way-ull, she has a big old farm over thar." Spit. "She has a little place out back she lets me live in." Spit. "I hep her with chores." Spit. "My place is nice, painted white." Spit. "I have a bedroom and a little TV set." Spit. "I have a double hot plate to cook dinner and a small Frigidaire." (Pickle-sheimer seemed really pleased about a *double* hot plate.) Spit. "She lets me have a garden plot right outside my door." Spit. "And all the farwood I need." Spit. "And one of the finest chicken coops for eggs and fried chicken you ever saw!" Spit. "Shiiiit, I don't reckon I need no Wesley Mountain Village." Spit. "But best of luck. You seem like a nice young feller." Spit. (As an aside, Picklesheimer's articulation of "shiiiit" was as artfully and expressively done as any rendition of it since Unca Clarence said it to me four decades earlier when I was crying in his driveway.) There were chuckles from his buddies and head nods, as if Picklesheimer had expressed some eternal truth that resonated with all of them. I responded, "Picklesheimer, if I ever met a man who don't need what I'm selling, it's you!" They all laughed, and I went on my way.

I contrast Picklesheimer's decision with that of my mother. Several months after my father died, she called and said she needed to talk. I went to her home, a post–World War II subdivision with two bedrooms and a bath and a half, on a quarter acre. It was our family's first and only home. It was furnished and decorated to Mother's tastes, including a world-class collection of plastic grapes draping wall sconces and picture frames. Our home featured art that included paint-by-number pieces; a hutch displaying Saran Wrap–covered, silver-plated trays, water pitchers, and a tea service; and numerous pictures of me and every girl I ever took to a school dance. Down the short hall to the small pine-paneled den and the two bedrooms was a modest bookcase holding the complete set of

Funk and Wagnalls encyclopedias through the 1965 annual update, the year I graduated from Avondale High School. The den included a foldout couch, a television with rabbit ears, and an ancient Singer sewing machine, plus an ashtray for Daddy's Tampa Nugget ashes. "Mamie and Da's" house was six miles from where I lived, a mile from their church, a block from the grocery store, and a ten-minute ambulance ride to the local ER. Most importantly, Mother lived on a street where neighbors Tuggle and Annette, Doris, Frank, and Sarah Helen were close at hand. Tuggle (a family doctor) and Annette, Tuggle's nurse and partner, had saved my daddy's life on more than one occasion. Doris and Mother were especially close friends. Over the years, our neighbors became known as the "Hamilton Road Gang," which included my friends who mostly went to the Belvedere Methodist Church and school together. Baseball and football in the street, hide-and-seek well into darkness, water balloon attacks on passing cars, and backyard barbecues were all common rituals.

Robert Moore, a lifelong John Deere executive, along with his wife, Elma, and their five kids, were the social coordinators on Hamilton Road. Their oldest son, Bobby, and I were very close friends, and still are to this day. Mr. Moore was a towering figure. He took us fishing, taught us how to shake hands like a man and cook hamburgers on the grill, and orchestrated a snipe hunt in the woods behind our subdivision. The Hamilton Road Gang was there for each other. Covered dishes when illness struck. Frank always made *the* best cornbread and still does, well into his nineties. Surrogate parenting when one family of three kids lost their mother to suicide. Celebration of baptisms, graduations, marriages, and funerals. Even financial help when hard times occurred.

So, when I visited Mother at her request, I was surprised and touched by her announcement to me that she was moving into Wesley Woods Towers. I was CEO of the place, and she had not told me she was even on the waiting list. I asked her why, and she said it was none of my business. I asked her what prompted her to make such a big decision. She said she was "lonely and afraid." Daddy had died six months earlier, and even though they had a difficult relationship, they still had each other. She said, "I have friends at Wesley Woods. They do the cooking and cleaning. I can still keep my car, and it's close to my doctors at Wesley Woods Hospital and Emory. I can plant flowers in the garden area if I want to. And it's closer to y'all [meaning Kathleen, John, David, and me. In fact, less than a mile away.] And I can still do my volunteering with residents who are visually impaired. I've thought a lot about it, and it's the thing to do at this stage of my life."

And it was. The "gang" was dwindling. Her Belvedere church had all but died. The shopping center had become seedy, and she was vulnerable to crime and exploitation. In fact, a housekeeper she had come to trust stole Mother's credit cards and reaped hundreds of dollars in charged items before she was apprehended. At the height of its glory, the Hamilton Road Gang represented what I call the "power of community." Close-at-hand neighbors met, knew each other well, helped each other, raised their children together. The extended Hamilton Road Gang family included the churches we attended, the local scouting troops, our organized baseball and softball leagues, and Avondale High School, into which we were all funneled. Avondale created new community experiences for sports, music, clubs, and great teaching as a broader tract, which not only sustained us but gave us the opportunity to thrive. Yes, the Hamilton Road "village" was the core of a community atomic particle that made up the molecule of Hamilton Road: a dynamic, energetic, and productive place to live.

But Mother recognized that those glory days were over. She was isolated, lonely, and less able to manage a home. So, she saw Wesley Woods as a "new place" to call home, even in the midst of "all those old people" (while never acknowledging that she had joined their ranks.) Her church work was replaced by resident association committee work. Her covered dish orchestration for friends who faced crisis was transformed into volunteer reading groups for the visually impaired. Sunday lunch and holiday meal events were replaced by inviting guests to join her for a meal at Wesley Woods. Instead of driving to the mall and navigating large parking lots, the Tower's van could pick up and deliver at the entrances of popular shopping venues, her medical appointments, and her church. Instead of calling 911, she could pull her apartment emergency cord or ask the nurse that made rounds at the Towers to check her blood pressure or monitor her chemotherapy or post-surgery recovery in her apartment. She had all the care she needed for her cancer treatments and never had to move again. The power of the Towers community replaced the power of the Hamilton Road community in a new dynamic form tailored for seniors whose life conditions changed as the evolution of aging modified their lifestyles.

As I compare and contrast Picklesheimer and my mother, I would say that we admire Picklesheimer's power of autonomy, and we would admire Mother's gravitation to the power of community.

As we grow older, we inevitably experience the tension between our personal autonomy and our need for community. Some will defend their autonomy to the death. I remember a son whose stroke-impaired father needed to be in a safe senior community environment telling me that allowing his father to stay at home at all costs was more important than protecting his father's dignity. All the while, his father was being swindled by people paid to take care of him and manage his business affairs. I asked him, What happens to his father's dignity the day he has to tell him he has depleted his resources and has to apply to Medicaid and be admitted to a nursing home. He had never thought of the situation that way. He was prompted to delve into the action of round-the-clock paid caregivers, whom he discovered were using Daddy's checkbook to feed their families, and a stockbroker who was using Daddy's account to churn stocks for his personal gain. He also found questionable oversight of the proper management of Daddy's medicine. Moving his father to a senior community became an imperative: go in time to make friends, before medical conditions isolate you.

Choosing living arrangements throughout the life span presents ongoing internal deliberations around the tension between autonomy and community. Rural or urban. House on a lot versus a condominium. Apartment with a roommate versus a dormitory. Single living versus marriage. As we get older, however, we are more and more likely to need an orchestrated type of community that Mother found at the Towers. She could pull an emergency cord, while Picklesheimer depended on 911; Mother had meals prepared, while Picklesheimer had to use his own double hot plate; Picklesheimer had to pay his own bills, while Mother wrote one check every month; Picklesheimer had to seek out friendships and enjoyable activities, while Mother had many of both under the roof where she lived. And when it came to needing health services, Picklesheimer had to broker his own provider network and the means to visit those providers. Mother had access to whatever she needed through a system of care, parts of which were delivered to her apartment. And if Picklesheimer fell in his bathroom, it could be days before anyone knew his predicament, but if Mother fell, it would be known within minutes. I don't know what eventually happened to Picklesheimer. I hope his autonomy of spirit served him well for many years, but his community seemed to be limited to the Widder Jones, his buddies on the balcony, and his chickens. No doubt there were other partners to support his autonomy— family, church, civic club? But whoever was involved wasn't baked into his community fabric. It was à la carte and dependent on the circumstances and the availability of those who supported him.

Dear friends of Kathleen and mine live in a beautiful condo community. They are an urban Picklesheimer couple. Both have chronic conditions that flare up. They have great neighbors, one of whom is a nurse, who just happened to be home when a crisis occurred. However, 911 is the only other mechanism they can use, even when assistance needed is not an emergency. They have attentive children, one of whom lives in the condo with them, but she has a job and is not available twenty-four seven. They hire a caregiver for bathing, dressing, medical prep, and light housekeeping, a popular option for strong-willed people of autonomous spirit. The condo association provides for maintenance and utilities, and they can both still drive, which means church, local club membership, and meetings with friends at area restaurants are still accessible. Our friends have explored planned communities like Mother chose, but there have been problems with every option they have pursued. This is the quandary that many seniors face: there is no place quite like home; there may not be enough privacy in a planned community setting; the decisions to be made are often irreversible; and the economics may not work. Yet, there are many seniors like Peter's mother who don't know why they didn't move into a place like Goodwin House sooner.

Others decide to move in with family: the spare bedroom, an in-law suite, an addition to the house. This has advantages as long as there is good health and good family relationships. A grandparent living in the home of working children can greet the grandkids when they get home from school and help with evening meal prep or carpooling. However, privacy can be compromised, and if dementia sets in, incontinence and sleep disorders attendant to brain deterioration can become a major disrupter to family routines and harmony. Families can tolerate disruption to family lifestyle with an elder in the home, but inability to control bowels and bladder and roaming in the middle of the night become circumstances of multigenerational living that most families cannot endure.

All too often, deciding to move to a senior community comes too late, usually after a crisis. Mary and LeRoy Smith were a retired clergy couple. He was blind from birth but a top-tiered scholar and musician. She was a church educator. They never served large or prestigious United Methodist pulpits back in the 1950s and 1960s because their bishop told them, "Brother LeRoy, no church wants a blind preacher!" LeRoy and I became good friends. He confessed to me that his blindness was nowhere near the difficulty for himself or Mary that people's attitude about his blindness was. Mary and LeRoy retired, prompted by her contraction of ALS (Lou Gehrig's disease). LeRoy had plenty of Picklesheimer pride, and they insisted to friends that they wanted to stay at home. Until. Until one day she was behind the wheel of their car and she lost control of her arms and hands. Fortunately, no one was injured, but their pride had metastasized into recklessness.

Clergy friends appealed to Wesley Woods to admit them to our campus on a priority basis, which we did. Mary had to be placed in our highest-level nursing home. (Remember, it was just a short time ago that she was driving an automobile, transporting LeRoy to his church obligations.) LeRoy moved into independent living after a brief stay in our lower-level nursing home.

They were a significant charitable care obligation, but donors rallied, and LeRoy began a transformation of his ministerial career. He was a paid evangelist. He taught voice, piano, and violin. He did fund-raising for charitable care contributions through personal testimonial. He wrote two books. And he chaired the religious activities committee at the Towers, which planned religious events and worship services.

LeRoy and Mary were mentors in the student chaplaincy program connected to multiple seminaries. Their faith was palpable. Mary was asked more than once if she was mad at God for making her sick. She exclaimed her response: "Of course not! What a silly question! Jesus Christ doesn't make people sick! He helps them ultimately get well!" Instead of driving in their previous hometown, they were regularly seen on the Wesley Woods campus, Mary the eyes of the duo sitting in a wheelchair, as LeRoy functioned as the legs of the two of them, powering along sidewalks and trails.

A new chapter in life for LeRoy began when Mary died. LeRoy missed her dearly but continued his work and met a woman whom he had known as a girl from his youth at the State School for the Blind. Her name was Ruby Shaw. She lived at Wesley Woods as well. After graduation from the school, they went separate ways and married, but both lost their spouses. Their old flame was rekindled and stayed so until both passed well into their nineties. They died fighting for a continued life of contribution to friends, church, and community.

All the above stories—Picklesheimer, condo couple, Mother, and LeRoy and Mary—illustrate four common approaches to living the last phases of life as we age, as well as precipitating factors that drive change in lifestyle. But each of them illustrates the need for community.

Picklesheimer, we can assume, had enough personal ingenuity to put together a home plan that he thought ideal. Many seniors do the same, whether at their long-standing homes or arrangements with friends, neighbors, and family. I assume the economics worked for Picklesheimer, probably because bartering with Widder Jones was involved and he raised some of his own food.

My late Unca George, of the earlier detailed BBQ sandwich fame, had a relationship with two friends in the poor mill village of Palmetto, Georgia. George could drive and had the biggest pension check. An elderly woman neighbor had a washer and dryer and did laundry as well as some cooking. Another male friend had a garden and chickens and could still do yard work for himself and his two friends. George drove each of them to appointments and events, including frequent trips that his male friend needed to make to the post office and liquor store. And they looked in on each other nearly every day.

The weakness of this organic community is that it is most often disrupted by health crises or accidents. Mary and LeRoy were no doubt supported by organic community until a near disaster made them move into a planned senior community, a move they fought until the day they moved to Wesley Woods. They had to have known that Mary behind the wheel of a car was dangerous to them and others, but the barriers of pride and denial clouded their better judgment.

The condo couple lives in a safe urban setting close to any service or convenience they could require. But their patchwork of neighbors, daughters, and paid assistance cannot bridge emergencies where time can be of the essence. While 911 is a great service, it is expensive and requires precious time for response. Condo couple dreads the nuisances of downsizing and the angst of deciding. Likely for them, a health emergency will eventually make their decision for them and their daughters. This is perhaps *the* most common decision-making mechanism at the disposal of all of us as we age. Once a health crisis occurs, the local EMS, Medicare, Medicaid, insurance plans, and hospital discharge planners dictate our paths and destinations. Under this planning scenario, it is all the more important to have legal documents executed and close at hand because any number of parties can take decisive action on your behalf whether or not you like the choices they make for you.

Mother's approach was more assertively planned. She faced the reality of the change in her circumstances: she was alone, and she knew the organic Hamilton Road Gang mechanism was crumbling. So, she chose her next move and entered a planned community that compensated for many of her losses. The power of a planned community saw her last five years of lifeways satisfactory to her and to her family. It also fit her personal economics, perhaps surprisingly so to many. Mother was a lower-middle-class socioeconomic consumer. She had slightly too much money for Medicaid but too little to live in a more luxurious environment. She was middle-class poor. Importantly, Mother, as well as Mary and LeRoy, made life transformations by finding ways to generate instead of stagnate and prove their lives had purpose till the very end. They also maintained an autonomous spirit even in a planned community. In fact, all three of these people were often a nuisance to professional management because they refused to be overregimented by rules and the convenience of the staff. Mother became the head of the loyal opposition party to the administration. LeRoy was a comrade-in-arms.

These four stories also illustrate the hidden enemies of healthy aging and a lifestyle that supports it.

Enemy number one is a tie for top spot: social isolation and clinical depression. Each can cause the other, but it's a deadly mix either way. I read a medical journal report years ago that asserted that undiagnosed and untreated depression may be *the* biggest reason seniors visit their doctors. Ike's story is the poster child for a quest for cancer as a cause for ill health when depression was the culprit.

Enemy number two: safety hazards. Bathrooms and kitchens are the most dangerous places, along with automobiles. Slips and falls at home are major villains.

Enemy number three: mismanaged medical care, including too many medicines, as reflected in the woman living at home who was taking fifty-two different meds every day. All had doctor and clinic names on the bottles. This did not count alcohol and over-the-counter meds.

Enemy number four: poor nutrition. Causes can be attributed to loneliness: "I don't feel like cooking just for myself," as many an older person has told me; or poor dental care, which steals appetite and causes infections; and loss of taste buds, which is the reason that sweets can become more attractive. My late Ain Lena nearly died from internal bleeding caused by a steady diet of *only* rutabagas and Geritol. When I asked her why she dined on those two items exclusively for a long time, she replied, "Way-ull, I love rutabagas, and I read in one of them magazines that Geritol has all the vitamins I need." (I suspect the alcohol in Geritol was an influencer as well, but I didn't pursue it.)

Enemy number five: mismanaged finances and uncoordinated service delivery. Most people today will retire with insufficient funds to care for themselves in old age. Alzheimer's alone has a shocking price tag. Many of us mistakenly assume the government will take care of us. More money is spent out of pocket than through public programs like Medicare and Medicaid. The existing government programs are very good, but too much is spent on institutions and drugs and too little on meals and transportation. Charlatans abound around vulnerable seniors' pensions, social security checks, and tangible assets like jewelry and silver. While some of the fraud is from companies that cheat Medicare, the bulk of fraud is perpetrated by family and so-called friends. This is why I have a bias about planned community: "those places." Yes, there are bad ones that do not deliver good quality and value for the money. But many serve an important role in generating the power of community and as a protector of watchful oversight. Below are the ten things to look for in choosing a really good planned community:

1. Reputation—Ask around. Locals know the good ones. Then visit before there is a need to do so. Then while there:

2. Trust Your Senses—Ask yourself what it looks, feels, smells, or tastes like. The odors of fried chicken and hot biscuits are preferable to urine and cleaning solutions. Check for basic cleanliness and obvious décor upgrades and well-kept grounds.

3. Look for Ant-Farm Activity and Residents with Attitude— Good places are abuzz with goings-on like exercise classes in a specially designated room, notification of trips, worship on-site or church bus pickup, support groups, or upcoming education classes like the one I saw in one place, "Best Sex Positions with Arthritis." The more modern ones have pools

and fitness centers. Make sure there is a beauty salon or even a spa. Ask about the most interesting residents who live there and chat with a few.

4.   Observe Resident-Staff Interactions—Natural, friendly inter-changes, including laughter, are a good sign. Meet the executive director, and if there is healthcare, the director of nursing.

5.   Ask about Access to Food and Dining Options—If meals are prepared on premises, eat there. If not, ask how residents procure food and if local grocery vendors and growers have a periodic market on premises.

6.   Ask about Access to Health Services—A services coordinator is a bottom-line must, especially in independent living communities. Health clinics for monitoring health conditions or posthospital treatment are a great sign. It is desirable if these activities are formally connected to a physician practice, hospital system, life plan community base, or health plan.

7.   Ask about Emergency Response—Each community should have plans for events like cardiac arrest, fire, flood, and criminal activity.

8.   Identify Who Owns and Governs—Nonprofits are preferable because they are governed mostly by local citizens who are volunteers. Their names are public record. Ask how often the board meets and what kinds of reports are generated about quality, finances, and human resources retention and turnover. Ask to see an audit.

9.   Interact with Staff, Paid and Volunteer—Ask staff how long they have been there and why they work with seniors. Notice

the availability of volunteers, youth and adult, and inquire about other community engagement like entertainment. Ask about staff turnover or retention stats. Ask if they use staffing agencies. The less dependency on contract staffing, the better.

10. Check Out Public Inspection Results—These are public record and indicators of quality.

In summary, why would any of us seek out a planned community as we age? Simple; they offer a network of services that contributes to health, safety, and vitality to reinforce our autonomy within the power of community, the right ecology for the "good old age."

Epilogue

It is incumbent upon all of us to plan for exigencies in our lives, especially as we get older. We owe it to our families, friends, and society to take responsibility for ourselves, both practically and financially. We literally cannot afford to do otherwise. Government has the responsibility for the catastrophic things that can happen to any man, woman, child, and community among us. But it is our responsibility to follow the Mary Jordan example and save a portion, donate a portion, and tote our own burden to the extent possible, with human and divine help.

It is up to each of us to document the decisions we make to mitigate family conflict and guilt for generations. It is up to each of us to be adaptable and exude a good attitude about growing old: neither victims nor deniers be! Instead, it is up to us to exemplify perseverance, not stubborn pride. It is up to families, friends, and our community establishments to treat us with respect and be inclusive of us—even with our frailties and limitations. As reflected in the Psalms, "Cast me not off in the time of old age. Forget me not when my strength fails."

For, in the end, we are all part of a divine plan of living and dying called aging. We cycle in and out of life, not knowing what comes before or after—the great mystery, as Hohaus concluded. But we leave positive or negative impact as we act our part to "test the play."

A very demented man was admitted to the Wesley Woods neuropsychiatric unit for his incessant and incoherent babbling. A young chaplain intern tried to connect with him and others like him through religious symbols, which she passed around in a group therapy session. As symbols like rosary beads, menorahs, and crosses were passed, a cross was grabbed by this man, halting his babbling stupor and prompting this comment: "Behold, I am the Alpha and the Omega. I make all things new again," a direct New Testament quote.

And so it is, we hope our individual life helps make all things new as we grow old, as we have seen through the exemplars introduced in this book of hallowed-ground stories—eternal truths shining through the real and imperfect souls we call family.

To live, age, and die like many of the people whose stories I've told, is to plant our feet on hallowed ground often in hopes of a "good old age" for generations to come. We want to be close to loved ones; to say goodbye and I love you at every encounter; to have few, if any, regrets; to have left our influence on others; and to be surrounded by our possessions through well-documented disposal of what we have accumulated.

Resources

Butler, Robert M., and Myrna Lewis. *Aging and Mental Health: Positive Psychosocial Approaches*. St. Louis: Mosby Publishing, 1977.

Cumming, John, and Elaine Cumming. *Ego and Milieu: Theory and Practice of Environmental Therapy*. Piscataway, NJ: Transaction Publishers, 1969.

De Beauvoir, Simone. *The Coming of Age*. New York: W. W. Norton and Company, Inc., 1996.

Erikson, Erik H. *Childhood and Society*. 2nd ed. New York: W.W. Norton & Company, Inc., 1963.

Jordan, Vernon E., Jr., with Annette Gordon-Reed. *Vernon Can Read!* 1st ed. New York: Public Affairs, a member of the Persons Books Group, 2001.

Rowe, John W., and Robert L. Kahn. *Successful Aging.* New York: Dell Publishing, 1997.

Thomas, William H. *What Are Old People For? How Elders Will Save the World.* Action, MA: Vander Wyk & Burnham, 2004.